BROKEN

—BUT—

USABLE

BROKEN
—BUT—
USABLE

God Uses Imperfect People

APOSTLE MILTON ADAMS

BROKEN BUT USABLE
GOD USES IMPERFECT PEOPLE

Scripture quotations marked KJV are from the Holy Bible, King James Version (Authorized Version). First published in 1611. Quoted from the KJV Classic Reference Bible, Copyright © 1983 by The Zondervan Corporation

iUniverse books may be ordered through booksellers or by contacting:

iUniverse
1663 Liberty Drive
Bloomington, IN 47403
www.iuniverse.com
1-800-Authors (1-800-288-4677)

ISBN: 978-1-4917-6958-4 (sc)
ISBN: 978-1-4917-6957-7 (e)

Library of Congress Control Number: 2015911781

Print information available on the last page.

iUniverse rev. date: 09/04/2015

To my wife: Dr. Sarah Y Adams, for believing in and supporting me, my vision and dreams. For the many long hours spent editing, proof reading and adding to this manuscript. For pushing me and bringing out of me this new creation; but most of all I thank you for seeing what others didn't see; a broken but usable vessel.

To my father, Apostle E. Q. Adams for teaching me how to answer to the call of God by calling my name morning after morning, again and again. Your life was truly a reflection of the Father. Today I answer to God through your calls. R.I.P.

To my mother, Mother/Evangelist Elizabeth Adams, for birthing me into this world and treasuring in your heart the things that only a mother could see in a child. Your child shall reach many. R.I.P.

Contents

Contents

Introduction

"They cried to the Lord in their trouble, and He brought them out from their distress; He made the storm be still, and the waves of the sea were hushed" Psalm 107:29 (KJV).

Many peoples assume that the weather simply obeys the laws of science and storms come about because of it. But in all truth there could be other reasons and powers at work.

Knowing that the storm, which was about to engulf them, was due to Jonah's disobedience, "They picked up Jonah and threw him into the sea; and the sea ceased from its raging. Then the men feared the Lord even more" Jonah 1:11-16 (KJV).

Jonah's disobedience had resulted in the storm, and when he was thrown overboard, the Lord silenced the storm.

When the apostles woke Jesus up, "He woke and rebuked the wind, and said to the sea, 'Peace, Be still! Then the wind ceased, and there was a dead calm" Mark 4:37-39 (KJV).

Storms come in three forms: spiritual, mental, and physical

In a storm, in another part of the Mediterranean, when all others on the ship had given up hope, Paul was able to stand up and make known that he had been told "There will be no loss of life among you, but only the ship" Acts 27:20-22 (KJV).

There are also symbolic storms in our daily life. When the enemy's planes flew into the twin towers in New York on 911, many in the United States felt the impact of this storm. There are storms that can hit our places of work, homes, families, ministries and lives. Suddenly all is in confusion. Some of you are facing storms, financial, death and divorce. There are also mental and spiritual storms that engulf us and our families. Some of the toughest storms are when a family is being torn apart and is in danger of breaking up by the force of the wind.

We are always in one of three positions in life. We are either going into a storm, already in a storm or coming out of a storm. Storms are sure to come in life and because of them many have either lost part or all of their faith in the Lord as a result of getting hit with such severe setback. Unless you have a full understanding and full knowledge as to why storms come and the purpose of them, you can have your faith in the Lord shaken to its very core depending on the level of power and severity of the storm.

Some may ask, "What is a storm, its purpose, and what causes it?" Well, a storm is an atmospheric disturbance, a disorderly outburst, which is being manifested in a violent commotion that occurs because of a change that has taken place in the atmosphere. This change is called season. If there were no changes there would be no seasons. Therefore, storms are violent seasonal disturbances that occur at the end and beginning of each new season.

Storms indicate that a change has taken place; a new season is coming and the old must go.

You cannot enter into a new season without going through a period of violent commotions and disturbances.

The reason is because the new season is a direct violent assault on the stronghold at hand. The old season, this stronghold, refuses to leave; therefore, a battle is at hand to force it to depart.

The Bible tells us that God's people are destroyed for a lack of knowledge. By not having the right kind of knowledge to fully understand why storms come in this life, especially to believers, can cause you to perish in your own personal dilemma. This is the very intent of the enemy.

Your personal trials can cause you to lose faith in God and that is exactly what the devil wants to see happen. If you ever end up losing your faith in God, like I did, not being able to fully understand why such severe adversity hits you in the first place, the result can cause spiritual death and leave you torn, broken and uncertain about life. This is the enemy's wholehearted, unreserved plan. His total, unrestricted, without limit plan is to cut you off completely from God through spiritual death and he will use any means necessary to try and bring this about. He will set you up to lose! When a severe storm hits, people are so often focused on the brokenness of the storm till they can easily miss the benefits of the storm.

There are benefits in every storm.

By not understanding this truth we fall for the bait that has been set by the enemy to entrap us. The enemy uses the severity of your brokenness to entrap you. God uses the severity of your brokenness to advance you! God will use it for your good.

The first question you will ask when you are hit is, why? Why me? Of all the people in this world, why did this happen to me? How can a good and loving God allow me to get hit with such a severe trial of calamities? How can God allow one of His own, especially the ones who are faithfully serving and following Him to get hit by something that literally came right out of the pit of hell? Well, at least you're right about one thing; it came directly from the pit of hell and the devil is using it to set you up for failure. It's a setup; however, the Lord is using what the devil brings in order to get you to the place where He desire for you to operate.

The devil focal point is not you, but God. It is his intent to paint a picture of God as being a God who allows bad things to happen to those who love Him. He distorts things to mean something that they were not intending to mean by altering the focus off of himself, as being the enemy and tries to direct it toward a God who is unloving and uncaring. This is the same deceitful scheme that the devil used from the beginning to setup Adam and Eve into sin, which caused spiritual-death.

A storm is an atmospheric disturbance, a disorderly outburst, which is being manifested in a violent commotion that occurs because of a change that has taken placed in the atmosphere.

Setup

Setup is a well-planned out strategy for a projected course of action by distorting something so it seems to mean something it was not intended to mean through the act of deception. The devil is a master of deception. He always leads away from truth. Though he means it for your bad, God has also predetermined it to be for your good.

The setup that the devil has planned for you is the same setup that God has purposed to get you to your destiny. Your destiny is a predetermined event that will happen. Trials and tribulations are the tools that God uses to get you there.

Trials and tribulations come with both a purpose and a reward. Everything has purpose and a reward, good or bad. The Bible says, "Consider it all joy, my brethren, when you encounter various trials, knowing that the testing of your faith produces endurance. And let endurance have its perfect result, that you may be perfect and complete, lacking in nothing James 1:2-4 (KJV). At the same time, we must be careful never to make excuses for our trials and tribulations if they are a result of our own wrongdoing. However, be it a trial as the result of your own doing or from another source, you can rest for sure that trials are your path to destiny. You are being made to win.

My destiny was discovered through different experiences of my personal life, trials and brokenness. It is my intention to help shine light on your path to perfection by sharing my path to destiny through life's experiences, hardships and troubles, with a focal point on how you are setup by Satan to lose, but made by God to win. You may be broken right now but God can use what no one else uses. Once you discover God's destiny for yourself, you will gain strength in growing through your brokenness by having an understanding of God's strategy to create a winner by using a broken vessel.

The term 'growing through' is used because if you are to go through, you might as well grow in the midst of it. And I must say, "I have grown." Read prayerfully and remember that there's no setup that Satan has designed that God hasn't already prearranged to get you to your place of destiny. You were born to lose, but made to win. Dance! You can dance in the storm. Don't wait for the rain to be over because it might take too long. You can do it now. Dance! Wherever you are, right now, you can start, right now; this very moment. Dance! Life isn't about waiting for the storm to pass, it's about learning to dance in the rain with your broken pain.

THE BOOK OF ADAMS

CHAPTER I

Why Didn't My Birds Sing Yesterday?

2 Peter 1:19 (KJV) "We have also a more sure word of prophecy; whereunto ye do well that ye take heed, as unto a light that shineth in a dark place, until the day dawn, and the day star arise in your hearts"

I dreamed that I was traveling on a bus with a group of people; some I knew well while others were strangers to me. Night slowly approached and darkness fell quickly. For some strange reason the bus stopped operating in the middle of an open field. One of the young ladies that were traveling on the bus stood and expressed in a raging voice, "I'm leaving, and I am not going to stay with this bus!" As she began to exit the bus, a bolt of lightning flashed across the heaven. From the light of the flash I could see a violent dark tornado forming in the distance.

I stated to those who remained on the bus, "We had better get out of the opening and run for cover." We exited the bus and began to run toward an old barn. Lightening flashed again and I could see the tornado fastly approaching. It was the biggest, ugliest, angriest looking tornado I had ever seen. I could see the blackness and violence of it as it twisted, picking up everything in its path.

One of the passengers and I ran into the barn and tried to open a drain near the foundation of the barn so we could hide beneath the foundation.

Unable to do so, we quickly ran inside, into a corner for covering as the tornado began to tear the barn apart. I could see the roof being lifted away from the force of the wind. Walls were sucked away. Though the storm was severe, for some strange reason there was no fear in me as I watched it shred the barn completely apart. I had peace in the midst of the storm.

As fast as it came, it quickly went away. For a moment there was total silence. All of a sudden, out of nowhere another tornado appeared, carrying away everything the first tornado left behind. I could feel its force pulling me. As it began to pull me, gently I placed my hand on a rafter to hold on. Again, there was no fear; peace in the midst of the storm. Moments later the storm was over. Two elderly women that were traveling with me, walked over to check on us. I asked where they were during the storm. They responded by pointing to an open white door in the side of the foundation of the barn. "We were there", they said. "Our safety was in the foundation."

Foundation is the beginning point, the basis and groundwork for anything.

Jesus said in Matthew 7:24-27(KJV) "Therefore whosoever heareth these sayings of mine, and doeth them, I will liken him unto a wise man, which built his house upon a rock: And the rain descended, and the floods came, and the winds blew, and beat upon that house; and it fell not: for it was founded upon a rock."

Suddenly, I remembered that others were traveling with me who never made it to covering. Quickly I began to run toward the place where I had seen them last. "Come quickly", I said to those who were with me, "Let's see if anyone made it through the storm!" As I approached the empty space of the open pasture I could see people looking for love ones. So many bodies without life. They were lined up on the ground, side by side to be identified.

As I came nearer I could hear people saying the name of the dead victims. I looked upon their faces but knew not a single soul. There next to a pile of brick I saw one that I could identify. In my amazement, as I came near, she suddenly opened her eyes, irritable about who put her among the dead. Why look for the living among the dead? I asked her where the others were. She assured me that they all were well. From a distance I could hear the voice my sister Mattie shouting, "Milton, we're over here. Randy and I are okay. We survived the storm."

We Survived the Storm

In the midst of the storm that we are in, there is still hope for us, especially hope in our Lord and Savior Jesus Christ.

Psalm 31:24 (KJV) says, "Be of good courage. And he shall strengthen your heart, all ye that hope in the Lord."

Psalm 71:5 (KJV) says, "For thou art my hope, O Lord God; thou are my trust from the youth."

Psalm 146:5 (KJV) says, "Happy is he that hath the God of Jacob for his help, whose hope is in the Lord his God."

It is good knowing that no matter what you are going through, no matter what storm you are facing, there is hope for you in the Lord, for the present and there is hope for you in the future because God is able to bless you and sustain you even in the midst of the storm that you are in right now.

David said in Psalm 37:25-26 (KJV), I have been young and now am old; yet have I not seen the righteous forsaken, nor his seed begging bread. He is ever merciful and lendeth, and his seed his blessed." Yes, God is able to take care of us in the midst of the storm that we are in. If you want to survive the storm that you are in right now, you have to stay in the hands of God.

Has there been a time in your life that you found yourself in a storm simple because you did not want to listen to nobody? Because you wanted to do your own thing, and you did not want to listen. Now you have found yourself in a storm that it's going to be hard to get out of.

Provide 4:13 (KJV) "Take fast hold of instruction; let her not go: keep her; for she is thy life."

Paul was in a situation where he has told a captain of a ship that they should wait until good weather come to set out to sail. But because he did not listen to Paul's advice, they found themselves stuck in a bad sea storm. And because they are now stuck in a bad, and dangerous sea storm, they have now risked themselves and the ship for a shipwreck. But yet in the midst of telling them that they are going to be shipwrecked, Paul also tells them to be of good cheer because there will be no loss of life in the shipwreck. Yes, the ship will be torn apart, but no one will die in the shipwreck.

It is a blessing to know that no matter what you are go through, no matter what storm you may find yourself in, it is a blessing to know that you are still in the hands of God. You may lose your marriage in a divorce, but you are still in the hands of God. You may lose your job, but you are still in the hands of God. You may have your paycheck cut by the government, but you are still in the hands of God. You may not have enough money to pay your bills, but you am still in the hands of God. Your friends may be few, but you are still in the hands of God. Remember to stay with the ship!

In the dream I sat on a tree stump facing the rising sun. The storm was over! Night was quickly being overtaken by the breaking of a new day. Sunrays filled the sky as calmness overlaid the beauty of morning. Stillness filled the air; what a wonderful feeling to experience peace and calmness after enduring such an intense, life taking storm.

As I lay in bed I could hear birds singing. I thought it was elements of my dream. Then I realized, as I awoke, the birds that were singing was outside of my window. My dream flowed into my present setting. This was a prophetic moment! The sun was shining brightly through my window as I arose to view the beauty of the day. As I opened the door to the outside, birds were everywhere. They were singing and flying all over the yard. Never had I seen such a thing. I stood in amazement as I watched this marvelous sight. Wow, so many birds and so many songs.

Prophetic Word: If there are no birds singing in your life at this present time, don't worry, your spring season hasn't come yet; but it shall!

Just the day before, I was outside working in the yard and hadn't seen, nor heard one bird singing. Today they are everywhere. I want you to know that God can change your situation around over night! I asked myself, "Why didn't the birds sing yesterday?" The Lord spoke to me saying, "Because it wasn't spring time. It wasn't your season".

I pray that your spirit just received that revelation. You hear birds singing every spring.

We all hear it, but most of us do not pay it any attention. Most of us don't understand it because it's not in our language; it's a birdsong! I truly believe that birds were the first to make music on earth. They are saying in songs, "The night is over, the storm has passed away. The sun is shining, it's a new day." Have you ever noticed that birds don't sing during storms? They fly for covering. Birds disappear during winter season; they fly south. Have you noticed that birds always sing at the breaking of day? They don't sing at night.

Maybe you are in a storm or in a winter season. Rejoice during your winter season spring always comes after winter. If there's no winter in your life, there will never be a spring season. Day always comes after night. When your day breaks your bird will sing! An outpouring of rain always comes after a drought. So you are going through a drought now; your season of refreshment is sure to come.

When My Bird Stopped Singing

I recall the day when birds stopped singing in my life. Service was over for the members of Broken Chain Ministries; the ministry where I serve as pastor. What an anointed service! The sun shined brightly as we stood about talking and greeting one another. Little did I know that I was about to embark upon a long unexpected journey that had been setup by my God to get me to my expected end. It was setup for me to lose but it was destined by God for me to win. Thank God He's always in control!

The phone was handed to me as I continued greeting the church members. On the other end of the phone came the voice of my younger brother. From the sound of his voice I knew it was a serious matter. "Your twin brother, Melton, has been rushed to the hospital", he said. "It's very serious". He went on to explain to me how he had rushed to his bedside to pray and comfort him. I will never forget the feeling I felt when he said, "His body was very cold when they put him in the ambulance to rush him to another hospital. I could see fear in his face. He was scared."

Because my brother had no insurance, the flight for life helicopter was not used to fly him to a key hospital, which was over a hundred miles away from the small town he lived in. Instead, he was placed in the back of an ambulance for the long journey ahead. At the age of fifty, my twin had suffered a heart attack, causing a blood vessel to burst in his heart, and he was slowly bleeding to death. Randy said to me, "Pray, because the doctors said that he may not make it to the hospital.

A Prophet is someone who is a mouth piece for God who interpret or transmit His command. A Prophetess is a woman prophet.

He could live five minutes, one hour or he could die any minute. It's a serious matter that we are facing." I immediately stopped the church members and went into prayer. My mother had taught me that prayer changes things. Whenever we faced a life changing situation, we always prayed, and God always came through. After prayer I left the church. Upon exiting the doors of the church, a Prophetess came to me with a word of prophecy. She stated that God had saved my brother's spirit and soul and to prepare the family for what was ahead.

Early the next morning, we departed Milwaukee going to Mississippi. We didn't leave Milwaukee with the focus of going to a funeral. We left with the intention of gathering force with the other siblings in Mississippi, pray and rage war against the spirit of death. That's what the Adams did. We pray. We praise. We bind and loose and believed the Word.

"Truly, I say to you, whatever you bind on earth shall be bound in heaven, and whatever you loose on earth shall be loosed in heaven. Again I say to you, if two of you agree on earth about anything they ask, it will be done for them by my Father in heaven. For where two or three are gathered in my name, there am I in the midst of them." Matthew 18:18-20 (KJV).

This was the promise I was believing God for. These are God's words! They reveal to us the most eye-catching yet fearsome thing about prayer, and that is its authority. Prayer is a powerful thing. Prayer has already divided seas and rolled up flowing rivers, it has made flinty rocks gush into fountains, it has quenched flames of fire, it has muzzled lions, disarmed vipers and poisons, it has marshaled the stars against the wicked, it has stopped the course of the moon and arrested the sun in its race, it has burst open iron gates and recalled souls from eternity, it has conquered the strongest devils and commanded legions of angels down from heaven. Prayer has bridled and chained the raging passions of men and destroyed huge armies of proud, daring, blustering nonbelievers. We knew what prayer could do. We lived it! It was our life!

As a family, we had been here before. This was no new thing. My, mother had escaped the jaws of death, suffered severe strokes and God delivered. My baby sister once died and came back through prayer after receiving third degree burns over eighty percent of her body. Dad escaped the jaws of death with six-bypasses on his heart. He died twice, but prayer brought him back. My granddaddy Arthur died in a wheel chair one day as Mom and my Aunt Rose was putting him in a car, prayed and God gave him life again. Even I had escaped the jaws of death with a heart attack, died and was carried away into the heavens, prayer brought me back.

Fighting the spirit of death was no strange thing. We knew how to fight! Prayer put food on my daddy's table many times. I know what prayer can do! What I'm saying is not mere overemphasis quotes, this is historical fact in the lives of the Adams' Family. Prayer had done a great many other things beside these for us. Prayer is an awesome, mighty force in our lives. We will join forces and pray again!

Before departing Milwaukee that morning, the Spirit of God spoke to me saying, "Take your robe, you will need it." Though God had spoken, it was still my confession that my brother shall live and not die.

The trip to Mississippi was a twelve-hour journey by car. About half way there, we stopped for gas. The Lord showed my oldest sister a sign flashing "code blue" that suddenly appeared in the store's window. Returning back to the car she stated to us that God had shown her a code blue. In the medical field code blue is a term use to indicate a medical emergency when a person's heart stops functioning.

As we continued to travel the highways, all at once my heart became unbearably heavy. It was as if a part of me had suddenly disappeared. Unable to drive, I quickly pulled to the shoulder of the road. Tears rolled unstoppable down my cheeks. I knew my brother had departed this life. I said to those traveling with me, "He's gone". My bird stopped singing his song.

In the early morning hours we stopped and made a phone call, asking about my twin's condition. Randy stated to me that our brother has gone on to be with the Lord. The phone fell from my hand as I exited the building from which I had made the call. I didn't want to believe what I had just heard. Those traveling with me awaited the answer. "He's gone", I said. Confusion filled my mind. How can this be? There's got to be a mistake.

After hearing the news, Timothy, my youngest brother, ran full force across an open field crying and screaming. There in the middle of that open field he sat in the midst of sewage waste in the darkness of the night. Evelyn and I fell to our knees and prayed as our youngest sister, Darlene, walked about in a state of shock saying, "He's not dead; he's not dead." No one could believe it. We had faced death many times and had always won.

No Man Land

Now we were at a place where we had never been before; no man land for the Adams. This day it appeared that death had won the victory and we had lost the battle. Out of all of our prayers, praises, confessing the Word, pulling down strongholds, calling those things that were not as though they were, our brother still died! My heart was broken.

Has this ever happened to you? Out of all of our praying, praises, confessing the Word, pulling down strongholds, calling those things that were not as though they were, it still didn't happen? Through this experience I learned that God will say no, if no is in His plan to get you to your expected end. God will use whatever means He has to in order to get you there. He will say no! The question is, "Will you still trust Him when he say no?"

I have learned that you have to trust God enough to realize that our all-loving, all-powerful Father loves us and has our best interest at heart at all times. So when it seems that God says "no" to our prayers, we must trust Him enough to understand that there must be a good reason for it. And I must say that most of the time it is beyond our limited ability to understand it, but we still must simply trust God.

I have also learned that one cannot forsake God and stop serving Him because of His no. Disappointment is a dangerous, powerful thing. When we get the feeling that God isn't listening to us, and has said "no" to our prayer, we have a tendency to feel disappointed in Him. And when this happen Satan whispers to us, "God said He loves you, but He's not here." And if we allow that disappointment to harbor in our hearts, it can drive a wedge between you and God.

Allow me to also say that we need to also realize that the answer may not be "no," sometimes. God could be saying, "wait a while." God don't always answer our prayers immediately, sometimes there's a delay in the giving of the answer and that can be a hard thing for us to accept. The ability to wait for an answer is one of the marks of maturity. Be willing to let God answer in his own time, in his own way, and in his own power.

Upon arriving in Mississippi I went directly to my brother's room, sat on his bed in total darkness and cried. I was so angry with God because I was so disappointed with Him. I didn't pray nor did I talk to Him. We had done what the Word said do. Still he died! It worked for other family members, why didn't it work for him. He was my brother! Not only was he my brother, he was my twin. Part of me died that day. "Maybe this prayer thing isn't really what it claims to be", was the thought that raced through my mind. Maybe it's all a figment of our imagination. Is God really who He claim to be? I stopped praying. Besides, what was there to say? Who was there to listen? No bird to sing a song.

Prophetic Word: As being chosen by God you are more a target for Satan. He will work overtime in setting you up to fail with storms that the average person will fold under but you are not average! You will win because God has chosen you to win!

Many times we see God as a divine vending machine in which you deposit one prayer and out pops a blessing. But what happens when you put your money in a machine and nothing comes out? You get angry, you kick the machine. So it's not surprising that such a view of God and prayer leads to disappointment when God says no.

Is He Really The Christ?

John the Baptist, the voice of one crying the wilderness, looked a far off and saw Jesus, the Savior of the world approaching him. John's announcement to the entire world was, "Behold, the Lamb of God who comes to take away the sins of the world" John 1:29 (KJV).

Jesus enters the Jordon River and John baptizes Him. The heaven opens and John sees the Spirit of God coming down from heaven in the bodily form of a dove. God speaks from heaven. John hears Him say, "This is My beloved Son in whom I'm well pleased" Matt 3:17 (KJV). John experiences a Trinity unity with the Father, Son and Holy Spirit.

There was no doubt in John's mind and with the conformation of the Holy Spirit and God speaking from heaven, that Jesus was the Savior. This is the One! Months later John is placed in prison. During his captivity, during his time of aloneness, in the darkness of a cold, wet, jail cell, John lost sight of who Jesus was. There are times in life that the crises you are facing will cause you to lose sight and question your faith on that which was at one time so real to you.

Jesus visited me as a twelve year old boy. When doctors walked out and said, "There's nothing else we can do", God healed my sister, mother and father. He answered my prayers many times. But you can still lose sight of Him. How you may ask.

When you are going through, many times we are often more focus and have in view the things that causes brokenness, fear and pain. We see the problem, not the Provider. Whatever you keep before you will become bigger than your faith in God. As in the case with Peter when he got out of the boat to walk to Jesus on water. As long as he was focused on Jesus, kept Jesus in sight, He walked the water. Once he started looking at the waves and listening to the wind he lost sight of Jesus and began to sink.

John had gone through so much that he asked his followers to go, see and ask Jesus is He really the Christ. Jesus sent words back saying to John that the blind eyes are being open and the lame is walking. He told John that He was the Christ. Your crises can be so close to you that you can lose sight of who God is.

God uses your enemy to get you to your destiny. Your enemies are in God plan for your life!

A Plan to Lose

Now, I realize that this was a well thought out plan the devil had setup for me to lose, but praise be to God, He used it to get me to another level. When my twin died it was like my world was turned upside down. Why was that? I think part of it was because I had convinced myself by reading numerous scriptures and promises, through the Word of the Lord, encouragements from members of my family, that we were God's chosen family. I tell you, no one wanted to believe those words more than I did.

Well, I still do believe that God's hand is upon my family regardless of this disappointment and many others beside. I've discovered that being God's chosen one doesn't exempt you from life's disappointments, as a matter of fact it makes you more a target for the enemy. John was God's chosen one for Jesus. By being God's chosen, you will have storms and as a matter of fact, you are more a target for storms. Being chosen of God,

Satan will work overtime in setting you up to fail with storms that the average person will fold under. You have been picked out to be picked on!

When you are chosen by God, you are picked out to be picked on. Paul was chosen; picked out to be picked on. Moses was chosen; picked out to be picked on. You are chosen; picked out to be picked on! Apostle Milton is chosen; picked out to be picked on.

The storms of life will come. They are like the weather. As you enter a storm the winds cause things to change. When the wind starts to blow, skies get cloudy and gray and the sense of worry sets in when you realize that you really don't have control of the matter at hand. Everything begins to change, one wave after another. When one passes you over, and you try to breathe, another covers you again. Your fight to maintain appears to be only a vain attempt. It's like fighting a losing battle of madness as life throws you unexpected events you didn't plan for, things you cannot stop.

When you are in the storm, the wind is blowing and the rain is mixed with thunder and lightning, it's hard to stay focused because you can't see where you're going. All you see is your period of being beaten by an uncontrollable wave, an uncontrollable situation. You have a sense of need because now your weakness is seen and is being demonstrated in your pain and suffering. It is during these storms when you need help. It is during these times of tribulation when you realize your need for someone greater than the storm; someone to help you and provide for you and maybe even give you a miracle.

> *God is your storm designer. He's not sitting*
> *back waiting for the devil to do something*
> *so He can react to it. He's in control.*

God is Your Storm Designer

It is during the storms of life that you realize the benefits of having a relationship with God or you will have an awareness of your neglecting Him when times were good and you felt that you didn't need Him. When the sun was shining and the weather was beautiful, you were so busy that you didn't have the time to live for Him.

Storms will give you a wakeup call. Yes, the devil may have brought it, but it is always God who designed it for you. God is your storm designer. God has purposed every storm in your life to get you to your expected end. Even as it was with Joseph from the beginning, God was in control and God is in control in your life. Every setup by Satan was in God's plan to get Joseph to his place of destiny. God uses your enemy to get you to your destiny!

Your enemies are in God's plan for your life. He uses them! They will cause you to leave your comfort zone. If you are to ever get anywhere with God, and have water-walking experiences, you will have to get out the boat and leave your comfort zone. Comfort is anything that makes trouble or sorrow easier to bear; it is the feeling of relief and is free from pain or hardship.

A zone is a particular area of operation. A comfort zone is the safety of the house and the support of family, friends and people, being within hand reach of their support. A comfort zone is a place where you don't have to operate in faith – eat, drink and be merry.

What does it take to leave the comfort zone? Storms! Storms will force you to do something beyond your regular setting. You will never have water-walking experience with God in your regular comfort zone. It is God's desire that we experience His wonders. Don't be persuaded by those close to you. Get up and get out of your comfort zone!

What does it take to stay out of the comfort zone? First and far most you must keep your eyes on Jesus. He has to become your total focus point. Secondly, don't be moved by what you see or hear. You will see the waves and you will hear the wind; howbeit, it's only a season changing storm to get you to your expected end. Thirdly, burn your bridges because you are not going back.

Saved, but Almost Lost

Several months before my twin brother died; he was a crack addict. Daily he would smoke the white rock of addiction through a thin glass pipe, trying to escape the burdens and disappointments of this world. He was setup by Satan to lose; howbeit, he was destined by God to win! My brother lost everything of value he had. He lived his life in the hog pen of sorrow; stealing and borrowing from those that were close to him. Setup to lose!

Most of life's major decisions are always forced on you

His drug addiction drove him from the bedroom of his wife to the back seat of his old worn out blue work van. There he would spend many lonely nights with regret of morning, knowing he would have to face the same battle of addiction again and again. No arms to hold him near; no one to wipe his tears. Pain was an accepted way of life; loneliness was common place. I know because I once lived the life of a drug user, but glory is to God, He delivered me!

Loneliness and pain forced him from the back seat of a church pew one Sunday morning to the altar of mercy. There with his head hunched low, he accepted Jesus as his Lord and Savior. There he became a new creation, born again and free from his addiction.

Angels in heaven danced around the Throne of God because he who was once lost was now found. God's grace, mercy and love accepted what no one else wanted. While the angels danced in heaven, Satan and his fallen angels worked overtime to set him up to lose. He had given his heart to God and his sin debt was paid; however, his debt to the drug dealer was still due. Because of his debt and unable to pay it off, he was beaten, kicked and stomped unmerciful by the drug dealer's mob openly in the street. One month later he died.

Hell danced with the shout of victory. Little did he know that Satan's setup for him to lose was God's plan for him to win. Several days prior, while sitting in church, God spoke to my brother saying, "I love you so much that before I let you go back to the streets and on crack, I'll bring you home." Setup to lose; destined to win! The devil meant it for bad, but God meant it for good! God used the devil to fulfill destiny. As I look back, and think about it, it was never Satan's setup. From the beginning it was always God's setup for destiny to be fulfilled. God used the devil. Every plan that Satan has against you is in God's plan for you to reach your destiny!

*Every plan that Satan has against you is in
God's plan for you to reach your destiny!*

I was awaken again by the ring of the phone late one night. Little did I know that I was about to embark upon another time of pain and dejection moment in my life. Another storm! Wave after wave. On the other end of the phone once again came the voice of my younger brother Randy. Mattie, my middle sister, at the age of 47 was found dead in her bedroom from heart failure. Another death. Another soul taking the journey into eternity.

I know that death is unavoidable and certain; however, knowing this alone did not make it any easier for me to endure the loss of my brother and now my sister. Where do you find comfort? The only place I know is in the hands of Jesus. Death smiled as I dropped my head in sorrow. So young was she. "Too soon", my soul cried out.

When King David learned of the death of his son Absalom he cried, "O my son Absalom, my son, my son Absalom! Could it only be, I would die for you, O Absalom, my son, my son" II Samuel 19:1(KJV)!

I believe that nothing brings more joy to Christian parents than to see their children grow and prosper in Christ. This was the hope and prayer of my parents for their children. The Bible teaches parents to bring up their children in the way that they should go and when they get old they shall not depart from it. In other words, your godly teaching will bring them back to God if they stray.

As it was with many of us, my sister strayed from the godly teaching of our parents. She too became a victim to substance abuse. Then the greatest of all pain, death, gave us pause and we again were consumed by the madness of a lost future.

Even with her problem, I've never seen a person show forth the love and grace of God as she did; washing the feet of her siblings, sleeping on the floor, giving up her bed that they may be comfortable. A no name, no face, outcast was she.

She was the woman that was caught in the very act of sin and Jesus said to her, "Where are thy faultfinders?" There was none for we all have faults. Jesus said, "Neither do I find faults, Go and sin no more."

I believe that there are many of us who will fight with problems until Jesus come or until we die. Some of us will overcome and some of us will not. Thank God for grace. For it is by grace we are saved. Grace saves us and it will be grace that will help us make it.

A broken vessel with much hurt and broken pieces was she. Used and abused by many, not to mention all the church members and men. God said, "Enough is enough. You fought, struggled, and scrapped till the end, come home my child. My grace is sufficient!

CHAPTER II

How I Wish It Would Rain

Matthew 7:24-27 (KJV) "Therefore whosoever heareth these sayings of mine, and doeth them, I will liken him unto a wise man, which built his house upon a rock: And the rain descended, and the floods came, and the winds blew, and beat upon that house; and it fell not: for it was founded upon a rock. And every one that heareth these sayings of mine, and doeth them not, shall be likened unto a foolish man, which built his house upon the sand: And the rain descended, and the floods came, and the winds blew, and beat upon that house; and it fell: and great was the fall of it."

Three months after the death of my twin brother, my childhood sweetheart of thirty-two years and I separated, eleven months later we divorced. Separation was death; divorce was the burial. Again I faced death; another setup by Satan. My life was falling apart; another storm, another wave, no bird to sing a song. I felt like Job, before I could make progress from one storm I was hit by another.

Everything I had worked so hard for, and believed in, was suddenly gone; empty house, empty home, all alone, my heart was gone. How can you live without a heart? You can't. You only exist. The only way to live again is for someone to give you his or her heart. And if they are to live too, their heart must be strong enough to carry the both of you. If there was one person that I was truly in love with, it was my childhood sweetheart. The question was asked, "If you loved her so, why divorce?"

Life is filled with things we never dreamed or planned. Sometime when the game is on the line we simply miss the shot and we lose the game. You don't plan to lose, it just happens and major decisions have to be made.

Once on a medical show there was a documentary on a set of twins who were joined at the head. They had spent their early months joined together, so naturally a bond was created. Being joined at the head, their brains were able to share the same thoughts and feelings. They were a single unit.

The parents decided that their life would be better if the twins were separated. Upon examining and x-raying the twins, the doctor discovered that one of the twins' hearts was weak and the twin with the stronger heart was really keeping the other twin alive. If separated, the weaker heart twin would surely die. The parents thought about it. The decision was made to let them stay joined so both could live. Life would be hard, it would be a different type of lifestyle, but together they could live.

Months later it was noticed that the twins were becoming smaller and weaker. The healthy twin's heart was becoming weak from supplying blood flow for both bodies. His strong heart had become weak from the stress of carrying more than his share in life. No longer was his heart strong enough to keep carrying what was never designed to be carried. There are things in life that God never designed for you to carry. The only chance for the healthy twin to live was to be separated from its weaker twin. Such a decision could cause the death of the weaker one.

What a decision to be made. The parents were to make a major life changing decision. It's never easy to do so and for the most part it's always forced upon you.

Bewildered by the decision and without a clue on what to do, they said to the doctor, "Maybe it would be best for them to remain joined. They have lived together thus far, allow both to die together." Some would agree with the parents' decision and say it would be a happy ending; however, the question would be, "Would this be the right ending?" Just because something is good don't mean its God or right and if you are afraid of being lonely, don't try to be right because right can make you lonely.

After much thought on the decision that needed to be made, the parents decided to separate the twins so that one may live. Yes, it would be a great sacrifice; one would have to die so that the other may live. The doctors operated and shortly thereafter, the feebler heart twin died.

Some may say, "What a sad story." Truthfully, there is sadness here; however, in reality, there's never a win of anything without the loss of something. It's called, "winning by losing." In every setup that the devil has for you, you will lose something; however, your lost will get you to your blessing. There are hidden blessings in your storm.

Have you ever found yourself in that place where it appears that nothing good can come out of a bad situation? Have you ever found yourself stuck in one of life's storms, and no matter how hard you try, no matter what you do, it seems that you cannot make any headway? Well, we all have times like that! It may seem to you like the storm will never end and that there is no possible good that can come from what you are facing.

Thankfully, however, there is some good news for us from the word of God. While the storms of life are never pleasant, they do produce certain benefits in our lives that we would do well to make note of. "Now no chastening for the present seemeth to be joyous, but grievous: nevertheless afterward it yieldeth the peaceable fruit of righteousness unto them which are exercised thereby" Hebrews 12:11 (KJV).

Your lost will get you to your blessing.

Destiny Order

As in the case with Joseph, he lost much before he came into his expected end. He lost home, country, family, and friends, became a slave in a strange country, falsely accused and incarcerated. He was setup to lose, but it was all in God's plan for Joseph to reach his destiny. The Bible states that the steps of a righteous man are ordered by God. Your steps are ordered by God for you to get to your place of destiny.

The word that is mentioned in the Bible is 'ordered' just like the way you order your food in a restaurant. You order as much as you can eat. In the same way, God orders our steps and steps that we are able to take. God's word says, 'He orders every step'. 'The steps of a good man are ordered by the Lord, and He delights in his way' Ps 37:23 (KJV).

Have you noticed the way we plan things in our lives? Most of them do not happen at all. Sometime people are concerned about things that may not even come to pass. Still there are some who spend half of their time in just worrying about things that are beside the point.

The Bible says, 'A man's heart plans his way, But the Lord directs his steps' Prov 16:9 (KJV). Notice the word 'step'. Our God directs our steps. "Trust in the Lord with all your heart, and lean not on your own understanding; in all your ways acknowledge Him and He shall direct your paths Prov 3:5 (KJV). The key to unlocking God's direction is by acknowledging Him in all our ways.

When we are in God's direction, we are heading towards abundance. It may not feel like it, it may not look like it. But the Word of God says God's path drips with abundance. Don't let the devil talk you out of that word. Our God is not a God of lack. He is a God of abundance. His paths drips with abundance. All you want to be is, in His path. God's word is final.

Something Must Die

There can never be life except something dies. With the twins, one gained life, but on the other hand she also lost oneness with the other twin. Both twins lost something. One died physically while the other lost the life she had once known. Never had she been alone. Never had she been on her own. At least there was always someone there even if it was causing the death of the both of them.

During my time of separation, the walls were quickly closing in on me. Never had so much pain invaded me. Aloneness became commonplace. Sorrow was my best friend and tears were my drinking water. What do you do when you hit rock bottom? I had always preached, "You look to the Hill from which cometh your help." Now, I didn't even have the strength to look upward toward the Hill. Death knocked at my door. No bird to sing a song.

During these time, different days I had different emotions. In the beginning I had thoughts like, "Who would want me now or who cares now. I am a failure." The reason I felt like a failure was mainly because of the belief of the church. The church taught me, "Marriage is until death do you part", and many held it over my head. Well, neither one of us died physically, but if we had stayed together, I believe I would have because of the stress or we both would have because of other situations. No, we didn't die physically; however, we both did die in some fashion or another.

Fear and pain will cause you to do what you never dreamed you could or would do.

The Day I died

I will never forget the day when Apostle Milton Adams died. I can take you to the very place, the very spot where I gave up; life mattered no more. How can you win a lost battle? Everything in me came to a stop. I couldn't fight any more. Physically, I would crawl into bed in a fetal position, watching the sunshine come and go in my bedroom. No matter how bright the sun shined, the room was always dark. No bird to sing a song. The only place where I felt safe was locked away in an empty house.

Mentally, I was totally blank. I couldn't see. I couldn't hear. I couldn't sing; I had no song. I couldn't believe; I had no faith. I couldn't preach; I had no Word. The only thing I had was pain! No bird to sing a song.

Spiritually, I was stuck in nowhere, not knowing how to move forward and too late to go backward. Who can I share with? Whose arms will hold me? How can the emptiness of my soul be filled? I've fallen and I can't get up. "Please, someone heal me", was my cry. No bird to sing a song. Born to lose; made to win.

There's nothing nice about divorce. Two hearts that had become one now go their divided ways. No one wins! You may have won the battle, and you may have been the victim, but the war continues. As a matter of fact, in a divorce, everyone is the victim: husbands, wives, kids, mothers, fathers, sisters, and brothers, church members and all. Everyone are victims! And yes, you can do badly all by yourself; however, you always need someone to love you.

There's nothing like the feeling of not being loved or wanted. You hunger to see a smile, to hear a laugh, to feel a touch, to taste a kiss, to give and exchange spiritual thoughts in a physical act. Your heart hurts. Your faith faces a crisis.

During a time of a crisis things are very uncertain, difficult, and painful. You face a breakdown. You face a time when action must be taken to avoid complete tragedy. It's a critical moment; a turning point in life where life suddenly went from good to worse.

I can truly say that a crisis is nothing you plan for in life, it just happens. Life is like that. We travel through life seeking to get to a place we desire. Sometimes we make it, sometimes we don't. We are on a journey. As we travel we pray for grace as we gradually pass from one inexperience state to another. Will we make it? Only God knows.

In your crisis God is taking you from an inexperience state, into a state of mature awareness; from a state of worldly wisdom, self-confidence, and boy did I have mine, to a place of changes, fine tuning and making major adjustments in your life. You now journey into the unknown! Your faith is your sight. Faith got you thus far and faith will see you through. I am reminded of the Word that God gave me upon entering Milwaukee. He stated, "Faith got you here and your faith will see you through".

You had your life planed but didn't prepare for this type of crisis. Everything you've done was toward fulfilling what you "believe" God has purpose for you. You give your life for it. You sold out for it. You planned for tomorrow, but, no man knows what tomorrow holds. Tomorrow is the "unknown." Only God knows tomorrow!

When God called you the path you took appeared to be fine. Than in the midst of your journey it happened, you faced a crisis. Boom! Your faith comes under an attack. All of a sudden you don't see what you use to see! Confusion fills your mind. Paying tithes and offering and you're faithful. All your dreams fall apart. You ask yourself, "Why did God lead me this way", or, "Did God lead me this way"? You spent so much "time" in developing what you truly believed God had purposed for you and in a moment's time it's not what it was. You ask yourself the question, "Have I wasted time"? Let me assure you that your time is not wasted.

The Bible states that "The steps of a good man is ordered by God" Psa 37:23 (KJV). God may not have order the crisis, but you can rest assured that God will use it. As being a believer, God has ordered your path not your crisis! In all you ways, acknowledge God and He will direct your path.

When you can't go forward, take another path

I am reminded when God told Moses to lead the Children of Israel out of Egypt He lead them the "Long way around." God directed their path. Why? Because God knew what was ahead and He knew His people. God knows you and God knows me. God knew that the Children of Israel weren't ready for battle yet. If He lead them the easily route they would have faced the enemy and went back to Egypt. What's ahead of you is greater than what is behind. In your crisis, in your life, and the path you are traveling, YOU will have to make some major adjustments in order to get to the place where God will have you to go. In your life you can always expect to make tough decisions, for a sure they will come. Most major decisions are forced upon you. The question will be asked, "Shall I continue on this path or shall I turn and go another way? Will I waste time? Will I make my next connection on time"? The question is, "What do you do when you can't go forward"? You take another path.

God said, "Your time is already accounted for". Time is already in God's plan for you. However, YOU will have to make the decision to continue or take another path, not God. Before taking another path make sure you count up the cost. Are you able to pay for it? Once a decision has been made to take another path, you will have to made major adjustments in order to not face the same crisis again.

If a decision is not made at the right time, you could miss your path. You could go too far down a path that will lead to "nowhere"; however it's not wasted time, God said, "It's experience time." You will learn from it and be able to teach others what "not" to do. A ministry will come out of you mishap.

Once a decision is made, it's made. Be it right or wrong, it's made. Now you deal with it. You cannot spend the rest of your life looking back on a decision that's made if you expect to go forward. The path you choose may take you out of the way, however, your "out of the way path" will connect to your path to get you to your destiny. Your delays doesn't mean denied. You are still traveling. You will get there in time. In time means "on time", which could mean "before time."

Will The Pain Go Away?

Pain will make you do what you never in your wildest dreams thought you would do. I can recall once in life when things were so bad and the pain was so great that I took an over-dose of pills; saved only by doctors who were able to pump the substance from my stomach. All I wanted was for the pain to stop. Once I reached for my handgun to stop the pain; I was stopped only by the thought of creating more pain, and going to hell, and may I remind you that I was a believer during these times too.

Allow me to detour for a minute. Just because you are saved, born again, don't mean you will not be tempted during times of pains. All you want is for the pain to stop and many will do whatever they can to stop it, be it right of wrong.

I am the first to say, "Divorce is painful." There is nothing that will quickly take the pain away; it is something that has to be worked through, lived through and grown through. When you are experiencing divorce, you are dealing with grief, with rejection, with having your heart broken. Yes, you want the pain to stop; however, taking away the pain would make you miss out on the growing process which is so necessary to bring about real healing. And you might risk getting into a rebound relationship for all the wrong reasons.

Instead, this is the time to work on yourself and personal growth and stabilizing your life. The grief you feel is real, is normal and is a process that will eventually also help your heart to heal. It's ok to give yourself time to work through the pain. It's ok to give yourself time to work through the brokenness. Healing is a process. You will learn that you don't have to live underneath the weight of this change. You can learn to grieve and grow. The pain may never go away but God can take the hurt out of the pain and you can begin again.

When going through a divorce it's normal to feel that you still love that individual, and if you really did love that individual the feeling is normal because you gave your heart away and committed yourself to them. You took vows to love him or her until death do you part. Unfortunately, someone didn't keep up their end of the contract, and sometime we are not always able to deliver what we promise.

People break promises. You wish they wouldn't change their mind. But you can't make a person change their mind and you can't make a person do right, and besides, you wouldn't want to force them to change their mind nor do right. When you really think about it you want someone to freely choose to love you for you. Why you may ask. Well, it is because love freely given is real love. Real love has to come from the person's heart and desire.

I know that rejection and betrayal are painful. But, would you want a person back because they felt pressured to come back to you because of what the church would say, or for reasons other than love? Many today are in bad relationships, acting a lie as if everything is ok. Why do we do such a thing? Because we are afraid of what the church will say and believe me they do have a lot to say. No, never force a person back. In fact, what you rejoiced in when you were first married is that special person freely chose you and freely loved you. As much as you might want to, you can't make a person love you.

Rejection does not change who you are and how valuable you are.

One of the first issues I dealt with was the feeling of rejection. I had to learn that rejection did not change who I am and rejection did not change how valuable I am as a person or to God. Rejection was a choice I made. That choice did not determine my worth. I was still a person uniquely made; someone with purpose, talents, opinions and who could still be used by God to make a difference in this world.

Why do you feel rejection? You feel rejection because you feel cut off from people, and people will cut you off. Believe it or not, friendships change when a marriage breaks up. You get cut off. You lose some of your "couple" friends. You lose "church people." You lose "family members." People treat you different. If you allow it, people will make you feel left out and isolated. You feel depressed and the depression of rejection makes you want to isolate yourself.

Let's face it, for most of us, whether we get rejected in love, friendship, in work, or wherever, a rejection feeling is awful. Rejection tends to turn us inward in a negative way, causing us to feel unworthy, flawed, not good enough, unlovable, frustrated, confused, angry, and sad.

I encourage you today, in Jesus' name, fight the spirit of depression and rejection which is at the core and causes you to tell yourself that you are not worth anything, your life is meaningless, nobody cares about you, you may as well give up.

It matters not if you are saved or not, changes will come in life and Satan will set you up to fail. And just because you are saved doesn't mean you will not deal with these types of feelings. This is a tough place to live. Sin has changed the very intent of it. It was never created to be such; nevertheless, it is.

Sometimes you just want to exit this place and go on home. On the other hand, no matter how tough it is to live here among disappointments, sorrow, aches, and pains, we still find ourselves taking medicine daily to remain here for one more hour, one more day, or one more week. Life is something; don't want to live and too afraid to die.

Can anything good come out of a bad situation? Can a broken heart be mended again? Can a lifeless soul live again? Can that which is crooked be made straight and blinded eyes see again? Yes, everything that the devil has stolen from you shall be give back to you sevenfold.

The reality of the death of your marriage, the loss of your spouse, the rejection and betrayal, a broken life and dreams is huge! This is hard! But, let me say, "This crisis is one you can get through to the other side". You can begin again! God will use your mess! God will use your mishap. This loss is one in which God can bring hope and in which you can become strong in the brokenness.

As I have stated earlier, there is no quick way to get through the pain of divorce. Besides, you would miss the process of character maturity, the ways God will answer your prayers each day, the way hope and strength will grow slowly back into your life. This will build a stronger foundation in your life and in your spirit. You will discover new blessings, new treasures, and even a new you, if you are determined to live and love again.

We live in a fallen world and we will experience pain from other people. Some of the pain will be purposefully given, while other pain might be an accident. We all have been hurt by someone and some of us have not gotten over it. When this happen your pains can easily be filled with bitterness; bitterness over your ex and how they treated you during your marriage and after.

You try time and time again to forgive, but still find un-forgiveness in your heart over the matter. I am the first to say that it is hard to let go of hurtful things that have happened to you and I am also the first to say that if you don't let go it will cause you to stop living your life. Life goes on! Let it go! If you breathe bitterness you will become bitter. Whatever you receive life from; it is that which you will become.

And God breathed into the nostrils of man and man became what God was; a god.

Life has taught me that bitterness never hurts the person who hurts you. Bitterness is only hurting you! I had to learn to place people, and the hurts they've caused me, in the wounds that Jesus received on the cross for me. There's room in there for everything!

Jesus' whippings and beatings, He endured for us, are so big, you could fit everyone who hurt you and their pains in them. Put your wounds in the wounds of Jesus. Put your pains in the pains of Jesus. Life goes on.

Release the person who hurt you

When someone you care about hurts you, you can hold on to anger, resentment and thoughts of revenge, or you can embrace forgiveness and move forward. Everyone has been hurt by the actions or words of another. Everyone! Perhaps your closest friend criticized your abilities, or your spouse had an affair. It doesn't matter where it came from, these wounds can leave you with lasting feelings of anger, bitterness or even a feeling of settling of scores; however, if you don't practice forgiveness, you might be the one who pays most dearly. By embracing forgiveness, you can also embrace peace, hope, gratitude and joy.

Forgiveness is a gift you give to yourself. When you look at it, forgiveness is almost a selfish act because of the huge benefits the one who forgives receive. It totally benefits you to forgive others. One of Satan's greatest deceptions is to cause you to believe that if you don't forgive others, they will be hurt and in bondage. The truth is it really puts you in bondage when you don't forgive. The other person has no clue that you have un-forgiveness towards them. Do yourself a favor and give the gift of forgiveness to yourself. You will live in freedom if you do.

In all true, forgiveness is a decision to let go of resentment and thoughts of retaliation. The act that hurt or offended you might always remain a part of your life, but forgiveness can lessen its grip on you and help you focus on the positive parts of your life. Your flesh might not like this but forgiveness leads to feelings of understanding, kindness and compassion for the one who hurt you.

When you're hurt by someone you love and trust, you might become angry, sad or confused. If you dwell on hurtful events or situations, dislike filled with resentment, retaliation and hostility can take root. If you allow negative feelings to crowd out positive feelings, you might find yourself swallowed up by your own bitterness or sense of injustice. By doing so you spend wasted energy and time trying to hurt and destroy the other person.

Don't get me wrong, forgiveness doesn't mean that you deny the other person's responsibility for hurting you, and it doesn't minimize or justify the wrong. You can forgive the person without excusing the act. As a matter of fact don't forget the act. If a dog bite you once always remember, the dog has teeth. What forgiveness does for you is bring a kind of peace that helps you go on with life.

If you're unforgiving, you will pay the price repeatedly by bringing anger and bitterness into every relationship and new experience in your life. Your life will become so wrapped up in the wrong that you can't enjoy the present. You will become depressed and uneasy. You will feel that your life lacks meaning and purpose. You will lose value and enrichment. Let it go! As you let go of grudges, you'll no longer define your life by how you've been hurt. You will define your life by how much you have overcome.

How far you go in life will depend on how much you have overcome. Overcome is to struggle successfully against a difficult situation. Just the definition alone lets you know that overcoming is a fight, but you can win through Christ Jesus. The Bible states in 1 John 5:4 (KJV), "For whatever is born of God overcomes the world. And this is the victory that has overcome the world, our faith. Who is he who overcomes the world, but he who believes that Jesus is the Son of God?

You are not born again to be overcome by the world. God designed you to be the overcomer and overcome the world! Forgiveness can seem overwhelming, but you can overcome with God's power combined with your faith!

Dead Man Walking

A few months after going through so much, my grandmother departed this life; another death. Again I'm on the very same highway, stopping at the same stations, going to the same house, and sleeping in the same bed I slept in when my twin brother departed this life. I was a dead man walking. No bird to sing a song. Things were going so well for me in my life, and ministry and all of a sudden I found myself in the midst of so many storms, one after another. I lost everything!

Live For Me Until I Can Live Again

How do I bounce back? How do I begin again? Which path do I take to get back to the place where I belong; giving and exchanging spiritual thoughts with God; operating in the realm of the Spirit? Can a dead man live again? Yes, he can; howbeit, there's one thing for sure, a dead man cannot breathe life into himself. Someone with life has to give him life.

In the Bible a young boy laid dead upon his bed. His mother commanded the servant to saddle a donkey and take her to the man of God. Upon her arrival it was asked of her, "Is it well with thy husband? Is it well with thy son? Is it well with thee?" Though her son lay dead at home, her reaction was, "It is well!" The mother explained the situation to the man of God and told him that her son was dead.

(2 King 4:32-35 32. KJV) "And when Elisha was come into the house, behold, the child was dead, and laid upon his bed. 33. He went in therefore, and shut the door upon them twain, and prayed unto the LORD. 34. And he went up, and lay upon the child, and put his mouth upon his mouth, and his eyes upon his eyes, and his hands upon his hands: and he stretched himself upon the child; and the flesh of the child waxed warm.

35. Then he returned, and walked in the house to and fro; and went up, and stretched himself upon him: and the child sneezed seven times, and the child opened his eyes."

The man of God went to the dead boy's home and went into his room. There he laid his body upon top of the dead boy's body; hand in hand, face-to-face, mouth-to-mouth. He breathed into the dead boy's body his breath, his life. The boy lived again because the man of God gave his life to him to breathe.

In the beginning God created man out of the dust of the earth and breathed into his nostrils the breath of life and man became a living soul. Dead man Adam lived because God gave him His' breath. Whose breath was the boy living on? The man of God! Whose breath was Adam living on? God's! Yes, a dead man can live again if someone gives him breath. Whose breath are you living on?

After the death of my twin brother, the divorce of my wife of thirty-two years, and the death of my grandmother, my bird stopped singing. Winter came quickly. The sun faded away; darkness covered my being; spiritually and mentally I died. Who can give me life that I may live again? This was Satan's setup for me, to die spiritually, mentally, and physically; howbeit, God was in control!

A lifeless boy's body was pulled from a lake after being under water for several minutes. His arms flopped, his legs hung down, his head drooped; He was lifeless! Quickly they laid him on his back. There the rescuer pushed his head back and began CPR, placing his mouth over the lifeless boy's mouth, blowing his breath into his mouth. Afterward he would push into the boy's chest several times, causing the heart to pump blood. This he did for several minutes. Shortly thereafter, the boy began to cough and breathed on his own. He was saved.

Looking back at the situation, I now realize that the rescuer was living for the boy until he was able to live for himself. When one has died spiritually, be it from a divorce, the loss of a love one, or any matter, they need someone to live for them until they are able to live again on their own. Someone has to fast for them, pray for them, and read for them. They are unable to live on their own. I truly thank God for those who carried me during those times of complete darkness. It was their prayers that brought me through. It was their faith that gave sight to me and their spirits that gave me life. I live today because someone lived for me until I was able to live on my own.

Your Bird Can Sing Again

"Come to me, all you who are weary and burdened, and I will give you rest. Take my yoke upon you and learn from me, for I am gentle and humble in heart, and you will find rest for your souls. For my yoke is easy and my burden is light" Matthew 11:28-30, (KJV).

Does the phrase "rest for the weary" stir up in you feelings of want and desire? Desires to laugh, sing, and have peace? Going through the loss of love ones and divorces, worries seem to increase at least twice as fast as rest. Sometimes we can get physical rest, but where can we go to find rest for our minds. In the Scriptures, Jesus is saying yoke with Me and your bird will sing again.

How can a bird sing with a yoke around its neck? Doesn't the yoke burden it more? I know that the yoke can be confusing when you first look at it and yes it does sounds crazy to ask a weary person to take up a yoke and pull a load when they are already burdened. What is Jesus asking of me? Does coming to Jesus mean we will be asked to carry a heavier load than what we already have?

To understand what Jesus is saying, we have to understand what a yoke is and the purpose it serves. A yoke is not just a device connecting an ox to a load. A yoke is a crossbeam that connects two oxen to the same load, dispensing the weight between them. When Jesus invites us to take His yoke upon us, we do not lift it off His shoulders onto our own; we become yoked to Jesus so He can help us pull the load.

There are some things that God is not going to move out of our lives, but He will give us help to carry it. Jesus doesn't need our help to carry a load; it is us who needs His help because we can't pull our load on our own. The truth is, when we yoke ourselves to Jesus, He starts pulling the load that we have been trying to pull on our own. His strength is so great until that which was heavy becomes light.

When we yoke ourselves to Jesus, we don't pull half the load. Jesus carries all of the load because His strength is stronger than ours. All we have to do is keep in step with Him as He pulls. Go through the motion! He is taller and stronger than we are, and when we are yoked to Jesus our burden becomes easier and lighter because our burdens become His burdens.

I know from experience that when you are going through, you feel like you are carrying all of your burdens by yourself. For me, it was because I started concentrating on the size of my burdens, what I was going through, how I was mistreated, and misunderstood; by doing this I forgot to keep in step with Jesus. When this happened, I tripped up and the weight got shifted back to my shoulders and I felt all of life's burdens. That's how I died spiritually. Whether it is the burden of guilt, pains of a divorce, problems with people, nervousness about the future, insecurity, or all of the above, we are told to bring it to Jesus and willingly give it to Him. As we continue to allow Jesus to carry the weight, we will find the rest He promises and your bird will sing again.

A Teacher Called Life

When the words of Jesus ask us to "Take My yoke upon you and learn of Me", it brings a question to mind. What is Jesus asking us to learn? What would make me want to exchange my own known and familiar yoke for an unfamiliar one? I believe by far and for most of us it's religious teaching and belief. I have discovered that many of God's children are operating in error, believing it to be truth. Error is existence in what is untrue. It is an act involving a departure from truth. Truth is that which is true; that which conforms to facts or reality.

Many don't know the spirit of error. The spirit of error lives next door to the Spirit of Truth; a lie lives clear across town. A lie lives so far from truth until you will know it's a lie. On the other hand an error is so close to truth until you might mistake it for truth. Error operates in the "gray zone." It is not truth and yet it is not a lie. It's an error.

The spirit of error works best when there's an ignorance of the Word. One must know the Spirit of Truth if they are to know the spirit of error. The Spirit of Truth is the Holy Spirit. The "Spirit of Truth" is the spirit "of" the truth. In other words it is the Spirit that comes from the truth. Jesus stated that, "I am the Way, the Truth, and the Life" John 14:6 (KJV). Jesus is the truth that comes from God and is the truth of God.

I don't believe that people deliberately set out to believe a false word. I believe they are swept into it because of several reasons. First, they don't know the Spirit of Truth. Second, they are unteachable and third, they are unsubmissive.

When one is deceived, they don't know that they are deceived.

Because many don't know error, they live their lives in bondage, unhappy, unsuccessful, stuck in nowhere, going no place, believing they are operating in truth. When Jesus said, "Come to Me and I will give you rest", this is a promise. You will receive rest, and a place of comfort. Jesus is inviting us into a relationship of rest so that our bird can sing again.

It is so sad to say, but for the most part, many believers don't believe that they are saved unless they are living continually in a storm of always being unhappy. This is error and a trick of the enemy! Jesus said, "The enemy comes but to steal, kill, and to destroy, but I have come that you may have life and life to its fullest" John 10:10 (KJV).

In taking on the yoke that Jesus is talking about, He is offering us relief from guilt and most of all religious bondages. He is offering us rest for our soul, and an opportunity to go beyond our natural limitations. He is giving us an opportunity to enter into a place where in and of ourselves we could never reach.

By yoking with Jesus we can enter into the wonder of becoming a part of something greater than we are. As for me, I am now connected to wisdom and power greater than what I had before my divorce and the loss of love ones. Being yoked with Jesus, my burdens are spread in such a way that I now experience new freedom, and independence beyond any I have known. Jesus has given me a light of hope and comfort for my weary soul. You can have that same hope too!

If you notice, Jesus asks us to take up His yoke, after He has invited us into rest. He does not tell us to pick up our old burdens and carry them after resting a while from the heavy weight. He asks us to do something different here. He's asking us to take on His yoke and learn from Him. He is not saying for us to keep dealing with old life's burdens and religious bondages after rest. The old is gone! Jesus is trying to teach us something by taking on His yoke and learn to live.

Unlearning To Relearn

How does one learn? Learning is different for everyone. There's no one way approach that works for all people at all times. When a person learns something, it means that he adds to what he had before the learning. In other words he becomes more knowledgeable after the learning than he was before the learning. There's an increase in the person. God wants to increase you in the knowledge of His wisdom. There's an increase in me. I now have more compassion, more anointing, more power. I am bigger today than I was on yesterday because of this increase.

I have discovered in my life's walk that I had to unlearn many things if I was to learn new things. You cannot add new layers of information and knowledge to an existing foundation of knowledge and expect newness if the old foundation is improper teaching. It would be like putting new wine into old wine skins. The wine skin would bust because it is set in its ways and is not flexible. Mark 2:22 KJV "No one puts new wine into old wineskins; otherwise the wine will burst the skins, and the wine is lost and the skins as well; but one puts new wine into fresh wineskins."

You can only operate in what you know or have been taught. Everything else is hidden from you. Truth is there but you are not aware of it. I was taught that once married you had to stay with that person until death, no matter what the other person did. This is error! I believe that what Jesus is asking us to learn from Him has a lot to do with our learning abilities and the willingness to receive. Everyone cannot receive the teaching of Jesus. To receive from Jesus depends upon a person's time table for learning, and their learning stlye; what happen for one to learn.

What's hidden from a person at one period in their life may be revealed at another time in their life as it was with me. I have learned that it's not a healthy thing to remain in a violent and toxic relationship. Now let me make this clear, I am not telling nor teaching you to divorce. What I am saying is, "It is senseless being in a violent relationship where both of you are unhappy, hurting one another and making others around you unhappy". If you are to remain together at least be happy together.

There is a time when goodbye is the right thing to say. I have hugged many of people at various parties. Many times one or the other of us has said, "This isn't goodbye." We mean, "This isn't the end." We mean, "I count on seeing you again." And, "I won't forget you." Goodbyes are hard. So we say, "This isn't goodbye." But sometimes "goodbye" is the right thing to say, because goodbye doesn't have to mean "The End." The word "goodbye" could be a reduction of the old phrase, "God be with you." Therefore, "Goodbye" could be a word of hope and blessing to someone.

God's Wisdom

I would like to think of this as God's Wisdom, learned through experience. Wisdom also knows that a person cannot be open to life's experiences and learning, until they go through for themselves as it was with me.

When one closes oneself off from wisdom and experience, it is Jesus' call in how and when to reveal hidden mysteries to that person. It was because of my teaching, and I do thank God for my teachers and teaching, that this mystery was hidden from me. It was Jesus' call on how and when He allowed me to see because I had closed myself off from this wisdom and truly thinking I had to go through a storm that wasn't mine.

Rest: A State or period of refreshing freedom from exertion, mental and emotional anxiety.

It's Not My Storm

I can recall driving during the end of a storm once, when I came behind a truck on the freeway. As the water from his wheels hit my windshield, it temporarily covered my view causing me to lose sight. I had been following a truck that was also caught in the storm. Sometimes in life we are following people who are stuck in a storm, cannot see and believe others can see for us. As I followed this truck, my windshield wipers were turned to full power, and was just barely holding on against the oncoming water. I couldn't see in front of the truck, and I wasn't really sure where I was, so I stayed behind that truck thinking that at least he could see for me since it appeared to know where it was going.

This all went fine until the truck slowed down. As the truck slowed down I moved into the passing lane to pass. As I came beside the truck, the wind and water from its tires nearly pushed me off the road. I speeded up to pass. As I came out in front of the truck, I suddenly discovered that the storm was over. The storm I was going through was made comp;etely up from the spray of that truck's wheels. It was never my storm and I could have been out of it long before.

He who is driving must be able to see the way.

I learned that the reason the storm appeared to be so great was because of several things. First, I was following the truck to close and couldn't see for myself. Sometimes you are so close to a situation until you can't see what's going on right under your nose and will become angry with someone if they try to tell you about it. An old wisdom filled Church Mother once said, "If everybody is saying the same thing, you had better pay some attention to it."

Secondly, I was depending on someone else to see for me. If someone is to see for you, you had better make sure first, they can see. Secondly, they know where they are and thirdly, they know where they are going.

I can recall one night I was traveling with my baby brother. I was asleep and woke up in the midst of a storm. I sat up and leaned forward to try and see. My brother asked, "What are you doing?" I said to him, "I'm trying to see where we're going." He laughed and said, "You better pray that I can see because I'm the one who's driving." What a true statement to make, "You better pray that I can see because I'm the one who's driving." Well, at least he knew where he was going and we did make it through the storm; however, I didn't go back to sleep until we were out of it.

Thirdly, when we seek to pass and move on in life, sometimes the storm appears to become greater. This comes from two sources: Number one, the force comes mainly from what's causing the storm, as it was with the truck, and number two, from those who are also in a storm. When people are in a storm they want you to remain in one so that you can feel what they are feeling. They want someone to relate, and if you decide to move on they feel that you are wrong because they can't or won't move on.

Most of the personal storms in our lives seem like tornados when you are in them. Maybe it's someone else storm and you are too close to the situation to see otherwise. Many people are this way. They convince themselves to stay in the storm rather than move on into the passing lane and do something better. They live their entire life being unhappy, and weighed down from a storm and feel that it's God will for them. Well, maybe it is God's will for you and maybe it's not; however, just because you believe it's God's will for you to remain unhappy, don't think everyone else has to be unhappy with you.

If someone is to see for you, you had better make sure they can see and know where they are going.

I Heard A Bird Sing At Night

After going through difficult, and brokenness, I heard no birds singing songs. The only song I could hear was, sunshine blue skies please go away. My girl has found another and gone astray. O, I wish that it would rain.

Sitting under the cover of darkness one night, I sat on a park bench under trees, out of sight. With my head toward heaven I fought with all my might, praying that something wrong could be made right. From my left I could hear a sound so clear. It was the sound of a bird singing so near. Why was this bird singing at night? Was it because it could see a bit of light? I turned my head toward the direction from which it came; again and again it would sing. Could it see what I couldn't see, as I sat there beneath the tree? Was the breaking of day truly on its way? Was this to be my dawn of a new day?

The sun did shine so bright and clear. Now I hold it in my heart as it beats so near. Oh heart, oh heart, now I can begin again. With you inside of me, we will always win. Yes, I was setup to lose but created to win.

CHAPTER III

Stuck in Nowhere

Luke 8:22 (KJV) "Now it came to pass on a certain day, that he went into a ship with his disciples: and he said unto them, Let us go over unto the other side of the lake. And they launched forth".

Major changes did come into my life. Decisions that changed life as I once knew. Believe it or not, we all will have to face and make major life changing decisions. Notice, I did say, "We all WILL have to face and make life's changing decisions." It's the way of life. The thing about major decisions, most of the time they are forced upon us. It's not something we simply volunteer to make or do. However, they are decisions that have to be made in order to move to the next level in life.

I was once asked, "Apostle Milton, how do you know when it's time to make life changing decisions? To answer that question let's begin by saying, I don't have your answer for you. Only you have that. I can say as stated before, "Most major decisions are forced upon you". It's not something you are seeking, expecting or looking for. It just happened. However, for the most part the reason it happened is because we overlook or turn away from facing all of the warning signs in life. We overlook all of the advance notice that something bad is about to happen. It's like the warning sign in your car that flashes to give you advance notice that a problem must be dealt with. By ignoring the warning sign or changing the channel, doesn't end the problem. The problem is still happening. If the problem is not faced and solved, it will force you to make major life changing decisions latter; decisions that you were not expecting to make.

Most major decisions are forced upon you

There are things in life that you simply don't expect to happen. You're driving alone. The windows are down. Cool air breezes across your face. You are in the fast lane. Life is good. All of a sudden the tire blows out. You lose control and crash. It's one thing to lose control but to crash can cause death.

We all lose control or have lost control at one time or another. Control limits or restricts the happening or expression of one's self by managing and exercising power and authority over self. To lose control is simply releasing the restraints off of one's actions and expressions. This could be dangers. If control is not quickly obtained or regained, a crash is definitely going to happen. There will be a sudden, complete breakdown and failure in your life. This breakdown could and will cause death to you and others. It is the crash that could take you out.

When there's a breakdown in one's life there's a breaking down of those fundamental components, parts, and elements that keep you together. Marriages, jobs, families, finances, and relationships are all destroyed when there's a breakdown. Everything you worked for is suddenly dead. It exists no longer. And if major decisions are not made quickly, you will die too!

Expectation Taken Away

I am reminded of a cruise that Dr. Sarah and I took to the wonderful State of Alaska. During the cruise we were to experience the beauty of nature as we slowly creep through the narrow Tracy Arms Canal going from Ketchikan to Juneau. We had been promised by the cruise line that this would be an experience of a life time as we beheld the wonder of God's creation. It was said that the ship would be so close to the mountain-side that you would feel as if you could reach out and touch it as magnificent waterfalls flow from the over hangs of the mountain's clips. Of all the wonders the cruise promised to give, this was the one experience I looked forward to the most.

As we entered the Tracy Arms Canal, it was of a true the experience they said. What a beautiful breathtaking, active exposure of an event it was. Slowly the ship creeps deeper and deeper into the canal. With every turn of an upcoming bend presented another wonder of God's creation. Breathtaking waterfalls covered the mountain side. Rocks formed beautiful images created from the hands of nature. Ice formed upon the ocean as sea gulls landed to view the passing ship. What an experience!

I noticed as we moved forward that the ship began to move slower and slower until we came to a complete stop. Once stopped, the ship began to slowly turn around. The Captain announced that the pass ahead was too dangerous to continue. If we continue, ice had formed and the ship could get stuck and we wouldn't be able to move forward or backward. "When is it time to make a major life changing decision", you asked? Before you get stuck in nowhere!

Based upon this knowledge the Captain made the decision to turn around and go back out to open sea to continue the cruise. What a disappointment! Everything I had expected from the cruise line and the Captain was taken away from me in a moment of time. My expectation was taken away from me. How could the Captain make a decision like this without at least talking it over with me? Besides, I had paid over three thousand, hard earned dollars for this cruise. They promised me this experience. I had expectation!

Life doesn't always deliver what we expect but life will deliver

During this time of disappointment and anger, God took the time to use this experience to teach me a valuable lesson on a fact of life. God never waste anything. Yes, I was disappointed and yes, I did have expectation. A decision had been made that affected me upon which I had nothing to do with. My expectation was gone. The cruise line didn't deliver what they had promised!

How many times have you been disappointed in life because someone didn't or couldn't deliver what they had promised and decisions were made that affected you that you had nothing to do with? If you have not experienced such a thing as of now, keep living, life will surely deliver it your way. That's a fact of life.

God revealed to me that the Captain's decision wasn't based upon my expectation or the price I paid for the cruise. In life you will make a decision that's not based upon others expectation. Like the captain, it was forced upon him. His decision was made totally upon the facts that if he continued to travel the pass on which the ship were traveling, it was of a certain that he would lose control, the ship would crash and get stuck in nowhere. Lives would be lost! Maybe even mine. The decision was to live or die. The Captain made the decision to live.

Passengers were angry. Disappointment filled the ship. However, the Captain knew the outcome before he made his decision. He knew it would disappoint people. He's not well-liked now. People shun his presence. No one listen when he talks. He's an outcast. He was not able to deliver what had been expected of him. We all lost because of his decision. How does the Captain live in such a surrounding? Yes, his decision to live not only involve his life, all aboard the ship lived because of his decision. Howbeit, no one saw their saving, they only saw their lost.

People are often focusing so much on their lost until they can't see their saving.

When making life changing decisions one must realize that many will not approve, accept, like, or agree with it. You will not be well-liked if your decisions have an effect on the comfort of others or if it involves you not being able to live up to the expectation of a promise. Howbeit, your decision to live is not based upon the expectation of others. Your decision to live must be based totally upon the desire to live and not get stuck in nowhere.

When I was going through complex and trying times in life and ministry, there were decisions that were made that were not pleasing nor accepted by many, mainly by those who were close to me. I wasn't well-liked and people shunned my presence, especially my kids and those of the household of faith. I knew my decision wasn't going to be a pleasant one. It was very painful. Messages were preached from church pulpits to target my decision. Invitation to preach and run revivals quickly came to a halt. No one came to my aid but praise God; He was there all the time.

If there was one thing I tried to do regardless, was to please those that I loved the most; wife, children, friends, and of a certain the church members. It would be great if life was like watching a certain movie on TV. If you don't like what you're watching, or what's going on, you can simply change the channel. But allow me to say, "Changing the channel doesn't stop the movie." The only thing that changing the channel does is stop you from facing what is going on. However, the movie continues on. Life goes on with all its hurts, pains, and disappointments. One of my greatest challenges was to face my disappointments.

Facing Disappointments

Why is it so hard to face disappointments? They are for sure to come, but none of us likes facing them. We always want to go for and get the gold; however, life isn't all peaches and ice cream. I have discovered that disappointments are for sure to come in life. When facing disappointments and adversity, how we handle them is more important than the disappointments of others. If you pray to have disappointments removed and they are not taken away, then you can rest for sure that God got "something better." God knows that there is some benefit that can only be learned through tough situations, circumstances and through life's difficulties.

Through all the things I've had to endure in life, I can for surely say, "It was all for my good." I am the person I am today because of the tough disappointments, circumstances, and difficulties I have suffered. They all pushed me into my expected end. The clouds were dark. The bed was cold. The house was empty. Never had so much pain overran my soul. I wanted to die. I found hope only in the Word. The Word stated, "And we know that all things work together for good to them that love God, to them who are the called according to his purpose." (Romans 8:28 KJV)

What's good for you doesn't always feel good to you

I know what you are saying, "The word good is just plain unpleasant in the midst of disappointments." And I must say that you are right. Certainly there appears to be no good in a bad situation. How dare you mention "good" when a woman is without husband and children have to deal with the pains of a broken home? Where is the good in the midst of trouble? Believe me when I say, I too struggle to find answers". Paul is by no means telling us that everything that happens is good. Instead, Paul is saying that God uses the bad things for good. Like Joseph, standing before the brothers who had wronged him and declaring to them that God meant their evil for good, Paul is trying to get us to see the good in a bad situation.

When you are suffering, there appear to be no good. There is no possibility of the situation being anything different than it is perceived to be, BAD. The question is asked, "Why did God permit this to be?" Not only did God permit it to be, but that He also sees it as being good for you. Can you remember growing up; you were told that the worst tasting foods were "good for you?" Spinach, lima beans, liver, onions, and rutabagas' all was supposed to be good, but your childish mind only saw the bad taste. I thought that cake should be good for me because it was good to me. It didn't work then, and it doesn't work now! Yes, cake taste good, but too much is bad for you.

Good in God's eyes isn't always good to us because we lack His wisdom and vision. We want God to work things out for good for us NOW. After all, NOW is when I need a little "good" in my life. If there is going to be some good we want it NOW, but it doesn't always come now. We live in a drive-thru, pop it in, microwave world where everything is now and this is the way we expect God to be. But God's plan doesn't always work on our timetable. The "good" that God is working in us is on His timetable.

Go to Sleep

Going through this crisis I discovered that God can take the hurt out of the pain. He doesn't stop the going through nor the pain. God just takes the hurt out of it. How can this be in the midst of turmoil? The Lord taught me how to sleep in the midst of the storm.

Luke 8 tells the story of rest in the midst of a storm. It had been a long day. Jesus had preached to the people, and the day was over. They had finished their work when the Words of Jesus said; "Let us pass over to the other side." In layman terms Jesus is saying, "Let US go to the next level." It's time to pass over to the next level and in passing to the other side you and Jesus is not about to sink somewhere in the middle! Did you hear what Jesus said? 'Let US pass over', you and Jesus.

It may not be a safe crossing but it will be a safe landing. Your ride may be rough but your landing will be smooth.

The word "pass over' means to leave behind by crossing over presiding, supreme space. What is Jesus saying? Once a decision is made to go to the next level, you have to 'pass over' the pain and disappointment that it takes to get there. While we "pass over" we will have troubles in our lives. While going ahead of, leaving behind, overtaking and out doing the overruling supreme space, you have to learn how to ignore and disregard its effect to stop you. It may not be a safe crossing but it will be a safe landing. The ride may be rough but the landing will be smooth. You must remember that Jesus said "let US pass over". "Us" is a pronoun referring to yourself and another or others. In this case it's you and Jesus.

If there's one piece of advice I could give to you in your decision to pass over is, "Don't try to pass over if Jesus didn't say, 'Let us pass over.'" Make sure you have Jesus in your boat. It is dangerous crossing alone. The presence of Jesus will help you through your storm. Jesus is the One who will make sure your boat lands on the other side. We serve a Savior who is strong enough. He is able to get us to the next level.

Jesus is the anchor for your soul in the storm and you will need Him because in just a moment of time you can go from peace to panic, and the storm is sure to come. All of a sudden your life will crack under the pressure of the storm. Having Jesus in your boat is no guarantee of being spared from your storm; however, it's a guarantee you will land if He said, "Let US pass over".

Your ship is full. You are in a hurricane of heartache. It's a severe situation. But I got news for you. God has purpose for your storms. It is like ironing. God is ironing out the wrinkles in your life. God will use your storm to break you, like a wild horse is broken before it can be used. God is saddling you up. Don't buck against the storm. Ride the wave and go to the next level.

When the disciples were crossing over, Jesus was in the bottom of the ship, fast asleep on a pillow. We can learn from Jesus' sleeping. Is He sleeping because he does not care? Sometimes we feel like He doesn't care, when we are in our feeling. The answer is, "No!" Jesus is asleep because He's in control; He's in charge. He has power over. He's the commander! Your storm is in Jesus' hand, not in the storm's hand. Jesus said, "Let us go over to the other side." His Word never fails. Heaven and earth shall pass away but God's Word shall never fail!

Jesus also said that He was with us always. When we don't feel Him, He's still there! When we don't see manifestation, He's still there! When we can't hear His' voice, He's still there! Go to sleep and rest because He's there.

You may ask, "Apostle, why is it important to sleep?" When you sleep you can't hear the storm. When you are sleep the storm has no impact on you. When you wake up from sleeping everything is OVER! You heard nothing, saw nothing and felt nothing when you were sleep. When you woke up all you see is the aftermath. Go to sleep!

Now allow me to leave this last word with you. No storm is allowed to continue if God is in control. Your storm will come to an end. Jesus will tell your storm to stop. It will be a calming rush overtaking you before the last wave destroys you.

The Long Way Around
Exodus 13:22 (KJV)

17. And it came to pass. When Pharaoh had let the people go, that GOD led them not through the way of the land of the Philistines, although that

<u>was near</u>; for GOD said, lest peradventure the people repent when they see war, and they return to Egypt.

18. But GOD led the people about through the way of the wilderness of the Red Sea; and the Children of Israel went up harnessed of the land of Egypt."

As believers, we are a people of faith. We are called faith people. We live by faith. Our salvation is through grace by faith. We believe that Jesus is to return by faith. Without our faith it is impossible to please our God. We believe that He is and that He can do what He said He can do. Our faith is the substance of things that we hope for, it is the evidence of the things we don't see. Take away our faith, you take away our hope.

If there's one thing the enemy is sure to attack in your life, marriage, and ministry, is your faith. The devil never really wanted me, he wanted my faith. Your greatest battle is the good fight of faith. Your faith is your eye sight. It allows you to see what cannot be seen. Without it you have no vision. Your faith will come under an attack and face crisis and the enemy wants to take your vision away.

When a crisis came in Samson's life, the first thing the enemy did was put Samson eyes out. A blind man can't see where he's going. A blind man can't see who he's fighting. A blind man can't see what direction he's facing. He's surrounded by total darkness and the enemy operates in darkness. He's the prince of darkness. Darkness is his domain. Where's there's no faith, there's total darkness. Where there's darkness, there's bound to be a crisis.

The first thing I lost during my storm of brokenness was my ability to see what I once saw. I saw no marriage. I saw no happiness. I saw no ministry. All I saw was darkness, trying to feel my way through this uncertain time because of my crisis.

What is a Crisis?

A crisis is dangerous or worrying times that we face in life. It is a situation or period in which things are very uncertain, difficult, and painful. A crisis is also a breakdown period when action must be taken to avoid a complete tragedy. There's nothing the devil like better than seeing a believer breakdown during a critical moment when something very important is about to happen and you are at a turning point as you travel life's journey.

Life is a journey. We travel through life seeking to get to a place we call THERE. Where is there? You may not know where it is but you do know for sure it's not where you are now. We journey from place to place, level to level, gradual passing from one state to another regarded as more advanced. In this process God is taking us from an inexperience state, into a state of mature awareness; from a state of worldly wisdom, self-confidence, to a place of changes, fine tuning and making major adjustment in our life.

We are journeying into the unknown! Our Faith is our sight. Faith got us thus far and faith will see us through. I am reminded of the Word that God gave me upon entering Milwaukee. He stated, "Faith got you here and your faith will see you through."

You have your life planed. Everything you do is toward fulfilling what you "believe" God has purpose for you. You plan for tomorrow, but, no man knows what tomorrow holds. Tomorrow is the "unknown." Only God knows tomorrow! When He called you the path you took appeared to be fine. Than in the midst of your journey it happened, you face a crisis. Your faith comes under an attack. You don't see what you used to see! The house you believed God for another family moved in it. Paying tithes and offering and you lose your job. All your dreams fall apart. You ask yourself, "Why did God lead me this way", or, "Did God lead me this way." You spent so much "time" in developing what you believed God had purposed for you and in a moments time it's not what it was. You ask yourself the question, "Have I wasted time?"

Let me assure you that your time is not wasted. The Bible state that "The steps of a good man is ordered by God Psa. 37:23 (KJV). As being a believer, God has ordered your path! In all you ways, acknowledge God and He will direct your path.

God told Moses to lead the Children of Israel out of Egypt. He lead them the "Long Way Around." Why? Because God knew what was ahead and He knew His people. God knew they weren't ready for what was before them. If He had led them the easy route they would have faced the enemy and went back to Egypt. Your steps are ordered by God!

Going Out of The Way

As I stated earlier, on our cruise from Ketchikan to Juneau, going through the Tracy Arms Canal, the Captain made a decision to turn the ship around and go back out to open sea in order to continue our journey. Getting to Juneau on time was important. The wife and I had purchased tickets for a special event. Being last meant the loss of money and missing the special event. Turning the ship around, going back to where we were appeared to be going out of the way. As a matter of fact it appeared to be going backwards.

Sometime in life, it appears as if we are in a backward motion, back in the same place where you were last year. There's a word God placed in my spirit that gave me strength to move forward. You may be in a backward motion but you are always in a forward progress.

I can recall once while traveling from Chicago, going South, I used the Amtrak train. Once boarding the train and setting facing the direction I was going, I was ready for my trip. As the train pulled off I noticed that we weren't going south, we were going north. Little did I know that while we were in a backward motion we were always in a forward progress. The train was going backward in order to get on the right track going south. Backward motion, forward progress!

Going through the canal the ship could only move at a slow pace. Once getting back out to open sea the ship's pace was faster. Time was made up! Not only did we make it to Juneau on time, we were there before time.

You may be in a backward motion but you are always in a forward progress.

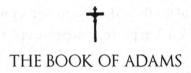
CHAPTER IV

Life Beneath the Snow

The phone rang one cold February day. I picked up to answer the call. On the other end was my sister, Prophetess/Pastor Evelyn. A word of prophecy was spoken saying,

"The Lord said, "Look out of the window. What do you see? The sky is dark and gray. The wind is blowing. Coldness fills the air. Trees are naked, standing as dead statues. Heavy snow covers the ground. No grass or flower to be found. No birds to sing a song. No sun to shine a ray. Everything seems dead; however, it's not what it appears to be. There's life beneath the snow! The grass and flower still lives. The tall leafless naked trees still lives. Though they appear to be dead, they still lives. There's life beneath the snow!"

Today you are covered, heaviness weigh you down. No life to be found. No sun to be felt. No arms to be held. Even as the tall dark trees stand naked and leafless, it's live. Even as the covered grass lives, you live! There's life beneath the snow. Your spring season shall come and your leaves shall return and your bird shall sing a new song. There's still life beneath your snow."

When a crisis comes in one's life everything around you gives the impression of being dead. I can personally say, "Divorce is a hurting experience." It will interrupt your life on every level, from ministry to work, to your social life, to your physical health. Well, that is if you were truly in love with the one you were married to. Life seems to come to a complete stop. No sunshine. No happiness. No bird to sing to a song. The wind blows bitter cold air; your tree stands tall, naked and leafless, while snow covers your flowers and grass. Everything appears to be dead; however, life is still going on.

There's life beneath the snow.

The journey to healing after tough times is a long one, and it is not easy. However, if you are to move on in life you have to face what has happen and deal with it on every level; from family, to children, to ministry, to friends, even to enemies. When a person goes through a painful experience, regardless of what it is, it's important to get back in control of your life and emotions; life doesn't stop, it goes on.

To move on in life, it is a must that you stop seeing yourself as a victim. Seeing yourself as a victim will always cause you to ask the question, "Why me?" or "What did I do wrong?" You didn't have to do anything wrong, things just happen in life. On the other hand you could have done something wrong, that happens in life too.

As being a believer we do our best to live holy and according to God's Word; even in doing so we still miss the ball sometime. The best you can do is all you can do with the hand you've been dealt in life. Remember, you may not win every hand, but you can get the best out of every hand and that's all you can do. Play the hand you are dealt.

You must realize that you are responsible for your destiny. No matter how the circumstances may have treated you, it is still up to you on how you will go forward. You can't go through the rest of your life with this guilt feeling on your shoulders. It is up to you to decide whether you will learn from this, be it a mistake or not, or whether you will be crippled by it. Life goes on.

You are responsible for your destiny.

Part of gaining control and moving on in life is by restoring and maintaining a positive self-image of you. Whether you are the one that initiated the situation or not, the feelings of failure can overwhelm your sense of whom you are. Well, let me serve you notice, "You are still a child of God and you have not lost your value."

Its church people that make you feel worthless. Your worth is still the same! A diamond ring in sewage waste doesn't lose it value! The sewage water doesn't change it value. The situation you are in doesn't change your value. You are still worthy the same after a divorce as you was before a divorce.

It is very important to keep feelings in perspective. Feelings is just that, feelings. Don't put yourself down; what is done is done, and it cannot be undone. You have to learn how to going forward and stop comparing yourself to others, stop trying to please people. You cannot please your haters! Stop trying to defend yourself and above all believe again, because you will always become what you believe.

Follow and Believe

There are two important things I had to do if I was to begin again. First, I had to keep following Jesus, even when I felt many times He wasn't there nor caring. You might ask, "Why keep following Jesus when He doesn't seem to care, you call and He doesn't respond?" Well, let me ask a question, "Why did you follow or call on Him in the first place"? You called because He had something you needed. The answer is very simple, "He still has what you need!"

A need is not a want or something desired. Need is an essential or necessary to something. A need is used to indicate that something is required in order to have success or to achieve something. If you don't get it, you will not succeed. If I don't get what I need from Jesus I will not succeed because He and only He has what I need!

Some may say, "Apostle, I'm following Jesus because I love Him." Well, again allow me to serve notice. Neither you nor any of us will be following Jesus if there weren't any benefits. If there weren't any benefits in doing right, we wouldn't do right. If the rewards were the same for right and wrong we wouldn't do right. As we follow Jesus we learn to love

Him; however, we follow Him because we need Him. He has everything we need to succeed.

Secondly, I had to believe in myself again and see myself like God sees me. We follow Jesus because He has what we need; however, following Jesus along will not get you what you need. He knows what we need; however, he wants to know what we believe. The reason is because what you believe is what you will receive and what you receive is what you will become. What you get from God is not based upon your needs but according to what you believe. He is not so much concern about your needs as He is to your belief.

The question is, "What do you believe?" What do you believe God can do? Not only what can He do, what do you believe about you? Why is this important? Why is it important as to what I believe about me? It's important because, "You will never rise above the image of what you believe about you." You will always become what you believe about you! You have to stop believing that you are a failure, nothing and nobody.

> ### *You will never rise above the image of what you believe about you.*

I was watching TV one day when I noticed a judge asking a young 14 year old boy the question, "Who do you think you are"? The question was in response to the boy doing something he wasn't support to do. His answer in response to the judge question was, "I don't think I'm nobody." As I watched the show it was brought to my attention that the boy's behavior was based upon his perception and belief of himself. He believed that he was 'nobody' so his actions portrayed his belief.

When God commanded Moses to send spies into the land of Canaan, they were asked to bring back a report about the land to the people. Moses chose 12 spies, one from each tribe. The spies traveled throughout the land for 40 days and returned to the camp with pomegranates, figs, and a cluster of grapes so large that it took two people to carry it. "The land is flowing with milk and honey", they reported, "but the people who live in it are powerful."

The spies say that they looked to themselves like grasshoppers and so they must have appeared to be that way to the people of the land. What's the point here? The point made is, "The power to come to change things doesn't come from the outside, but from the inside". Your setting responds to what you put out from within. If you believe in yourself, others will believe. If you see yourself as a grasshopper, others will also see you that way.

You have to learn to believe in yourself and ministry again. I am what I am today because of what I believed about myself yesterday, and tomorrow I will be what I believe about myself today. Today is a reflection of what I believed about myself on yesterday. I believed I could become an author on yesterday; therefore, I am an author today. It is of a truth that you don't always get what you deserve in life, but you will always get no more than what you expect, because what you expect is what you really believe.

Expect is to confidently believe; to believe with confidence, or think it likely, that an event will happen in the future. In the natural when a woman is expecting with child she is pregnant with and look forward, future term, to the birth of a child. In order for her to be or get pregnant, she had to receive a seed. It is that seed that cause her to be pregnant, "expecting" a child. In the natural you will always give birth to what you are expecting with. In the spiritual you will always give birth to what you believe because what you believe is what you expect.

Believe is your seed to expecting

There were two types of spirits that came back with the 12 spies; the spirit of a fruit bearer, and the spirit of a grasshopper. Which are you going to be? I made a decision to become a fruit bearer. Let me explain to you what God revealed to me about what a fruit bearer and grasshopper spirit is. First, fruit bearer is a twofold word, "fruit" and "bearer". To fully understand what a fruit bearer is, we need to understand each word.

Fruit is the produce of any plant grown; the making, bring into being, or turn out of a plant. In layman terms, a fruit is the value or worthiness of the plant. A 'bearer' is someone who brings or carries something. The plant is the bearer. You are the plant. Together a 'fruit bearer' is one who carries the creation or making of itself. In layman terms a fruit bearer is one who carries its own value. You carry your own value by what you believe. What you believe is your fruit! Do you hear what God is saying, "You are carrying your own value by what you believe"! The fruit came from you. The fruit is the inside of you being manifested on the outside of you.

On the other hand a grasshopper is an insect that lives and feeds on the fruits of plants. It is a fruit destroyer. It takes away from the plant. A grasshopper is a fruit killer. In other words the grasshopper is a killer of the fruiter bear's fruits. Your worth or importance is not set by people or your situation. Your situation and people are grasshoppers. They have the spirit of destruction. They will destroy your worth and importance by destroying each and every one of your fruits. Yes there will be more against you than there will be for you. Ten spies were grasshoppers; two spies were fruit bearers; Joshua and Caleb. Which are you?

I feel lead in my spirit to also warn you that more people will believe what the grasshopper's spirit say, than what the fruit bearer's spirit produces. The children of Israel saw the fruit bearer's value; yet, they choose to believe the words of the grasshopper's spirit. What I am saying is, "Don't try to prove to people whether you are right or wrong. They will see your fruit and it's up to them to believe what they see or whether to choose and believe what they hear." Because the Children of Israel choose to believe the grasshopper's spirit over the fruit bearer's spirit a whole generation was lost and destroyed.

If you are going to be a fruit bearer you have to contain a positive image about yourself. You cannot strive for the approval of others to feel good about you. It doesn't matter what others feel about you, it's what you feel about yourself that affect you. You must base your image on what God says about you, not people. How you see yourself and how you feel about yourself will have a tremendous impact on how far you will go in life. You will never rise above the image you have of yourself.

You cannot base you importance on what other people have said about you, what your parents and siblings have said about you, because of your pass failures, or on what you have painted in your mind about yourself based on your accomplishments. Your value and importance must be based on and only on what God says about you. God says, "You are fearfully and wonderfully made."

Don't assume you know me by what you heard; I grow daily. Your messenger might have outdated information!

Fearfully and Wonderfully Made

Psalm 139:14 (KJV) "I will praise thee; for I am fearfully and wonderfully made: marvelous are thy works; and that my soul knoweth right well."

I was made to be who I am today. I wasn't born this way! There are many things in life that I have no control over or had nothing to do with. I had no control over being born; no control over being a male or being an Adams. I had no control over being an African American. I am here not by choice. I am here because I was made to be here. I was "made" to be me, and I am fearfully and wonderfully made. There's no other person on this earth I'd rather be than me. You might have a problem with me, but you can rest assured, I have no problem with me. When I say, "Made" I mean I wasn't born like this. Wisdom and life's experiences have made me. Made mean I have been built, constructed and formed into being. When something is made it is safe to say that there was a time when it didn't exist.

During divorce I died; a new me has been made. Therefore, special preparation came into being whom and what I am today. I was "specially prepared" to be me. Prepared mean I was made by a special process by being put through a special condition. In other words I was specially prepared by a special process of being put through this special condition in life. Therefore, it is also safe to say that going through what I've gone through in life has constructed and built me into being what I am. I can truly say like David said, "I am fearfully and wonderfully made." I have no regrets; life goes on and I go on with life.

Life has given me the true meaning of being fearfully and wonderfully made. Fearfully comes from the Hebrew word meaning not know what the outcome may be. What each person goes through affect each person differently. When I went into this earthquake of an experience I didn't know what the outcome would be, but God knew it would be wonderful. He knew the end before I went in. When going through life's tough times it's hard to see your end and that's fine. Just keep your eyes on God because He can see what you can't see.

Wonderfully comes from the Hebrew word meaning something so new and unfamiliar, so out of the ordinary, so beyond expectation that it excites a feeling of surprise, admiration, or something astonishing.

You don't know what the outcome will be, but it will be so new and unfamiliar, so out of the ordinary, so beyond expectation that it will excite God with a feeling of admiration that something marvelous is being made out of you. God knows that you will look much better after you come out than you did when you first went in. And when you come out you will discover that life keeps on going and you must go on with it.

How to Make a Cake

What makes a cake, a cake? Some may say, "It's what goes in the cake that makes it a cake; the flour, eggs, butter, flavor and sugar." Others may say, "It's the process; the beating & whipping." Others may say, "It's the fire; the heat transform it from one substance to another." In all true, it's all of the above that makes a cake a cake.

First it's a selection of special ingredients that has been selected for the cake; not by the cake but by the one who's making the cake for a particular purpose. Special ingredients have been selected by God for your life for God's particular purpose.

Secondly it's the process of being beaten and whipped. Even as the cake is whipped and beaten, life will also give you a whipping and beating. Before the whipping and beating there were many different separate ingredients. Whipping and beating will bring all the special ingredients together to form one substance. The Bible said that, "All things work together for your good." 'All things' means this plus that, plus that, plus that, all coming together to form one substance for your good. You will be able to say, "It takes more than flour to make a cake."

Thirdly, it's the fire; the fire transforms the cake from one form into another; from dough into an eatable substance. The fire will transform you from an unusable creation into a vessel fit to be used by the Master; from being what you were into what you are now. Ready or not life will make a new person out of you and life will never choose to stop because of you. Life goes on. God has selected special ingredients for you. If there's to be a new you the old must first die. It cannot exist anymore.

The new you have the faith and power to begin life again. The battle that the new you have is the battle of unbelief.

Luke 9:24 (KJV) "And straightway the father of the child cried out, and said with tears, Lord, I believe; **help thou mine unbelief**".

One of the most difficult things for me to do after divorce was to believe in love again. It doesn't matter how messy or how clean a divorce is, it's hard learning to love someone again. Your trust in any type of relationship is pretty much shattered and to put yourself back in a position to be shattered again is hard to do. Not only that but it's also very hard to break the emotional bond that you once had with your ex after years of marriage in order to move on in a new relationship. Removing or actually stopping that emotional bond will take time to heal and bring the freedom you need to move on.

Going through this crisis, there were much emphasis on faith and getting more faith. This sort of teaching left me thinking, "I'm not hurting because I'm lacking faith. I'm hurt because of brokenness".

Faith is not the problem. You are hurting because of a situation that occurred and decisions that were made, not your faith. When there's a problem, a strategy of the devil is to get your attention onto fixing the thing that's not broken. Your faith is not broken. Maybe your faith in another is broken but your faith in you is not.

If Christ lives in you, then there's nothing wrong with your faith. But you might have a problem with unbelief. You might have a problem with believing in a particular thing or person again. God is faithful and He will heal you, but unbelief will limit the power of God in your life to trust another relationship. So stop worrying about your faith, you already have enough to be healed.

You have enough faith to be healed and began again; however, faith will not heal a relationship that once worked at some level for you. Why? Because more than you is involved. Your faith is for you.

Your faith will heal you and you do have to be healed. Healing doesn't come by replacing one relationship with another. Healing comes from removing yourself from the emotional bond that caused the brokenness. You can learn to love again through hard work and trusting again but you have to go through the proper channels. Healing is the first step to loving again; overcoming unbelief in love is the second step.

If you are not healed from your past, you don't want to meet someone and their least behavior pattern is similar to your ex. You will pull away and not give that person a chance. Though the meanings are totally different, your feelings are the same. The reason is because you are not healed. When someone gets divorced, often times they build a protective wall around their heart. You want to make sure you are completely over that before you begin loving again.

Out of all your past hurts, disappointments, protective wall building, and distrust, there's something about the need to give and be loved again that will push you out of your safety zone; it is the need to be loved.

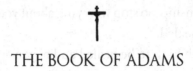

CHAPTER V

Purposely Called

Genesis 3:9 (KJV) "And the LORD God called unto Adam, and said unto him, Where art thou?

The wind blew fierce against the walls of the old shabby house as it moved willingly through every crack and hole to fill the room with bitter cold. The old worn shed had weathered many storms. The beatings of the storms had to a great extent appeared to have won the battle. A rat breeding, roach infected place was she, housing a share-cropper preacher and his poor struggling family. Times were hard, life was tough, and money was short. Many times meals were nothing more than flour gravy and flour bread.

Clothes were thin hand-me-downs that covered the bodies of this preacher man's children while worn out Mother Goose shoes covered their feet. Regardless of the condition, a sense of closeness filled the house as each family member depended upon each other for comfort and encouragement. Two or three would huddle close together in each bed at night to keep warm from the bitter cold. This was my family.

I can remember moving closer to the body of my brother, fighting the bitter coldness with the heat his body made available. The heater was turned off during the night to reserve money because of the high cost of gas. Each member of the family silently waited as the darkness of night faded away. Light began to move secretly into the room as daybreak. Warm sun rays shined through the window as we welcomed its presence.

God calls your name because you will say, "Yes".

Through the thin wall I could hear the movement of my parent's bed as my father called out to me, "Milton, get up and light the heater!" He always called my name! From beneath the cover I came forth, only to confront the bitterness of a cold filled room.

Across the room I could see the bed of my other brothers as they silently waited beneath their covering for me to respond to the call of my father's voice. In another room my sisters waited for the sounds of my footsteps rushing over the coldness of a frozen floor, racing to light the heater. My parents, whose room was closer to the heater, also waited. The entire family waited for my response to the call of my father.

Sleep filled my eyes as I struggled to obey his command. Of all days, why today? Why didn't he call someone else just once? It was only yesterday and the day before and the day before that and the day before that, which I was called upon for such a task. Why me? Doesn't my father know that there are others who could do the things he's asking of me?

Whether I hear my father's call or not depended on the condition of my ears, and exactly what I hear depends upon my spiritual attitude. Remove the thought from your mind of expecting God to come to force you or to plead with you. When our Lord called His disciples, He did it without tempting pressure from the outside. The low, yet passionate, firmness of His "Follow Me" was spoken to men whose every sense was open. If we will allow the Holy Spirit to bring us face to face with God, we will hear "the voice of the Lord and in perfect freedom you must be will to say, "Here am I!"

Bitterness filled my heart as I sat and thought within myself, he's always calling me. He calls me to shave him. He calls me to fix his coffee. He calls me to cut his hair. He calls me to go to the store. He calls me for everything. Of all the people who live in this house, and there were about eleven, he calls me again.

The question that raced across my sixteen year old mind was, "Why Me?" This is the question that always race across our minds when we feel that something improper has befallen us. Why does my father always call me? I would later discover that it was because of the position I had put myself in earlier in life trying to please everyone just to feel important.

As I sat in bed and thought on these questions, I could hear the sound of my father's bedroom door open as his footsteps raced swiftly across the frozen cold floor toward my bedroom. My heart pounded with fear, for I had not responded to his calling. Suddenly the door to my bedroom swung opened and there he stood. Everything appeared to go into slow motion as my father moved toward my bed. Quickly from my bed I leaped to face his anger. His voice was strong and very firm. "Boy, didn't you hear me tell you to get up and light the heater!?" he asked.

To obey is better than a sacrifice.

I had never rebelled, I had always responded to his call. Now I faced a situation that I didn't know how to respond to. "Yes sir", I said, "but I am not going to light the heater today, there are others who can do it too." What a mistake that was. From his right side it came. Fast and swift, a right hook that knocked me flat to the cold floor. My body was trying to get up but my head was saying, "Stay down." Stars filled my vision. Monkeys danced about my brain. Who turned out the light? You see, dad was the type of man that treated you the way you acted. If you acted like a child, he would deal with you on a child's level, but if you acted like a man, he would deal with you on a man's level. That day I acted like a man, got treated like a man, and was knocked out like a man.

From the floor, tears filled my eyes as they ran down my cheeks. Anger filled my heart. "You will pay for this", I said, as I fought to stand to my feet. From beneath the covers, my brothers raised their heads only to see a broken and angry boy facing the authority of his father. My mother raced swiftly down the hallway to see what was happening.

As she arrived she heard the words that fell from my father's lips. "When you can't obey the authority of the house, it's time for you to let the doorknob hit you where the good Lord split you!" I will never forget those words that day. Because of a rebellious heart, pride, anger and hurt feelings, I left the covering of my father's house at the age of sixteen to face a world I knew nothing about. My mother cried. My siblings stood in silence as I departed the house.

Many are called but only a few are chosen.
Chosen come to those who respond to the call.

My Hero, My Enemy

The one, who clothed, fed and loved me the most suddenly had become my enemy. How could this be, only the day before he was my hero? It was a setup and I was too young to see it coming. My focus wasn't on my disobedience to my father's command, but rather on the discipline action that had been applied. No doubt Adam and Eve felt the same way after their disobedience to God's command. They too were setup by Satan to think that God was their enemy.

On Sunday morning, April 15, 2007 at 4:57am, I was awakened from what I believe to be a prophetic dream. In this dream I saw what appeared to be the Empire State building in New York City standing high in the heaven collapsed to the ground. It appeared to be solid gold. From New York City the Spirit took me to London. There in London the same event was taking place. The Tower of London was also standing high in the heaven and it too appeared to be solid gold, and it too collapsed.

Prophetic: an accurately predicting or foreshadowing
of something that will happen in the future.

It was brought to my attention that New York City and London are the financial capitals of their countries. The gold represented the financial system of each country. I believe that was the collapsing of the financial system in the United States of America and England that have had an economic effect on the entire world as it is known today.

This economic collapse is a setup from the Middle East. It is a well-planned out strategy for a projected course of action to happen by deceiving the United States and England to make it seem to mean something it was not intended to mean through the act of deception.

The United States is the most powerful country on earth. Of all the countries to live in, I thank God for being a part of America. There's much that I disapprove of and disagree with in the government and operation of our country, but compared to other countries we are blessed; founded on God and godly principles. However, the one thing that troubles me the most about our country is the turning away from the godly principles and foundation it was founded upon.

God has become America's enemy. Prayer is no longer in schools and the name Jesus is not allowed. The Ten Commandments are taken out of our State Courthouses. The killing and abortion of millions of unborn babies cry loud from clinics and hospitals across our land while killings and violence over throws our streets, schools and college campuses.

Yes, America is the biggest and strongest country on earth; howbeit, I have also discovered that the bigger you are the harder you will fall. The Bible declares that a nation that turns away from God shall be turned into destruction. America has turned away and destruction is indubitable to come. History has proven to be true to this fact to all countries that has turned away from the Living God.

America, the great giant, is asleep to the fact that she's being setup to collapse by her enemy. The loving God that she once served has become nothing more than a mist of our imagination and our faith has become an obsession of the past. How do you over throw a giant who's more powerful, stronger and bigger than you? One thing for sure, you can't fight him face to face, power for power. You have to set him up to fall from the inside without him having an awareness of his downfall.

Daily I observe this truth being displaced across our television with the war in Iraq. There's no way that the small country of Iraq can win the war and overthrow America by fighting her face to face, power for power; she's much too big and too powerful. The only way she can be defeated is through deception. She has to be setup to loose and America has been setup by her enemy and you can rest assured that the United States of America will lose the war.

The strategy of the enemy is to hit where it hurt the most.

On 911 America came under an attack on her own soil from the Middle East, thousands of lives were destroyed, Americans were angry and afraid. Her sense of security was crushed. Home wasn't safe anymore. The enemy knew how to get in; howbeit, it was only a snare by the enemy to lure Americans away from their own land to fight a war on the home land of her enemy. While she's away fighting a war on her enemy's home land, her enemy is fighting and winning a war here in America. When your enemy is bigger and more powerful than you, you have to fight a smarter war than your enemy, if you are to win.

The strategy of the enemy is twofold. First, pull Americans away from their home land to fight a war on her enemy's land. By doing so, her focal point will be Iraq not home. The enemy knows that America will spend billions of dollars to fight this war. This cost will weaken her economy and every American will suffer through the high price of oil. Hit your enemy where it hurt the most, in their pocket.

The second and deadly strategy is to cause the Americans to turn against their leadership. After 911 President Bush was America's hero when he invaded Baghdad. Everyone didn't agree with the way he did it, but everyone agreed that something had to be done about it. Afterward, President Bush became the enemy of the American people. What a setup, pulling the focus away from the true enemy by turning the tide on their leader. This is the same strategy that the devil uses daily against the children of God.

The approach that Satan used against Adam and Eve was to come in the form of an angel of light by revealing to them that the God of Creation, their Father, was really a liar and was holding out on them. The real truth was that Satan didn't want them to be like their Father, a god. America is setup by her enemy to believe that their hero is their enemy.

I too believed that my hero had become my enemy. Leaving the covering of my father's house, I quickly ran to the streets for shelter. In the streets I learned the hard way that to obey was better than a sacrifice. I would pass the house in the wee hours of the night only to hear the laughter of my brothers and sisters enjoying the comfort of home. When

I was there it appeared to be nothing more than the norm, now it was the one thing I desired the most; I hungered after the voice of my father calling my name. Sorrow filled my heart as I vanished in the darkness of the night.

A Child Need It's Father's Blessing

Genesis 48:9 (KJV) "Joseph said to his father, 'They are my sons, whom God has given me in this place.' And he said, 'Please bring them to me, and I will bless them.'"

Now allow me to say that there's nothing wrong with leaving home once reaching the age of matureness; however your leaving must be proper. You need the covering of a godly father. If you can help it, never leave home without the blessing and covering of the house. You cannot build a good life on a bad foundation. It doesn't matter how far you may go in life; if the foundation you have built upon is not proper, it's only a matter of time before your life will crumple.

You may ask, "Why do I need my father's blessing?" A young man needs his father's blessing. If not given he will search desperately for a blessing and will put himself in all sorts of situations in order to get it. I've witnessed this in gangs and became a gang member in search of it. Kids get into gangs because they want to be accepted by a family.

When the Father calls, answer Him with a "Yes Father"

Most kids that get into gangs have no relationship with their father. No blessing upon their lives. So, as a result, they go into the gang, because the gang promises them that they're going to be part of a family. "I've got your back, and I'm going to watch you all the way, and I'm with you no matter what." This is the blessing the father is to bestore upon his son, not another.

Have you seen tattooed teardrops on a gang member's face? Those little tattooed teardrops stand for some terrible crime of death a member faced. Why? Because there was no father's blessing upon the child's life. Kids commit crimes in order to get into gangs. This is also their initiation fee. If they have to kill someone to get into the gang, they will do it, because they need to feel that they are part of a family. And only a father can make a child feel that way. A mother, by herself, has a hard time doing that. Most gang members love their mothers. It's their fathers they've got the problem with. They never received the father's blessing.

In Genesis 27 Isaac is blessing his son and Jacob steals Esau's blessing and his birthright. Four times in this chapter, Esau begs for his father's blessing, but it never came. The Scripture says Esau always hated Jacob for that. The emphasis is more on the blessing than it is on the birthright. The blessing always involves a hug and a kiss. Not the kiss of abuse, but the kiss of blessing, there's a huge difference.

It is important that young men hear and obey the voice of their fathers. Jesus put it in these words. "He who hears and obeys is like a wise man who builds his life upon a rock and when the storms of life come his life will stand because his life was built upon obedience." (Matt 7:24 KJV)

Without the blessing of my father, my life was without a covering. The streets were hard. Life was empty. My alone turned to loneliness. Loneliness became an unbearable pain, and pain will cause you to do what you never dreamed you would do.

Of all the things I have had to deal with in life, pain has been the greatest. I have searched and discovered that there is nothing to compare it to, not even death itself. My rebelling as a child came from the unwillingness to continue to deal with the pain of dying by denying myself in order to please my father. I wanted to do what "I" wanted to do.

Dominion is a created performance, while submission is a learned performance.

There's something about being your own man, and doing your own thing. What is it about being independent? In reality man was created this way. God created man to rule and have dominion over, not to submit to. Dominion is a created performance, while submission is a learned performance. Submit means coming "under" the authority of my father and I wanted to do things my way.

Sometime you may think you want something, but when you get it you find out it's not what you really wanted. I thought I wanted to leave home but the streets taught me that what I really wanted was to hear the call of my name from my father.

From the streets I came, returning to the house of my father. Drugs filled my veins. Brokenness covered my very being. Life had taught me a lesson that would last for a lifetime. Like the Prodigal Son, I remembered what was in the household of my father and asked for his forgiveness. Again he would call my name. Again I would have to respond. What a delight it was to act in response.

There's nothing like the voice of your father calling your name. Adam was driven from the presence of his Father to never hear his name called again. What a feeling, it was. Silent, aloneness, loneliness, I too can relate. I ran from the presence of my Father because of disobedience. Glory is to God that He called my name again. If you listen closely you can hear God calling your name again.

> ## *There's nothing like the voice of your father calling your name.*

When He Calls

Often times God doesn't call us for a task, as we often think He does. He calls sometimes only for fellowship, just to walk in the cool of the day with His greatest creation, giving and exchanging spiritual thoughts. God wants to be with you. He wants to have fellowship with you. He will call you just for lunch. There are times He calls to bring us under the shadow of His wings for protection, like a chicken calls her chicks when trouble is near. He knows best. He sees the enemy coming and summons us to come only to protect us. And yes there are times He calls us to give us an assignment. The one thing that you must remember is, when God calls, you must always answer.

Later in life I would ask my father, "Why did you always call me? Of all the children in the house you selected to call my name the most."

His answer was shocking, but delightful. "Because you would always respond", he said.

God calls you because He knows you will response

Little did I know that the call of my natural father would become the discipline training that would teach me how to act in response to the call of my Spiritual Father. I know how to respond now, my father, Apostle E. Q. Adams taught me that. Today God often calls me, again and again I response. Many times I would that even He wouldn't call my name. You must understand that in order to respond to any calling is the giving up of ones will, wants and desires, in order to bring about that which brings pleasure to another, even to God.

Yes, it is my heart's desire to please my heavenly Father, but I must confess that life's burdens, disappointments, pains and hurts sometimes make you want to walk away from the burden of your daily cross. Your flesh cries daily to come alive. It's for this reason there must be a daily crucifying of one's self.

To Obey Is Death

How does one resolve the struggle within himself not to die? How does one bear the pains of the cross by crucifying one's self? Paul said, "For that which I do I allow not: for what I would, that do I not; but what I hate, that do I. If then I do that which I would not, I consent unto the law that it is good. Now then it is no more I that do it, but sin that dwelleth in me. For I know that in me (that is, in my flesh,) dwelleth no good thing: for to will is present with me; but how to perform that which is good I find not. For the good that I would I do not: but the evil which I would not, that I do. Now if I do that I would not, it is no more I that do it, but sin that dwelleth in me. I find then a law, that, when I would do good, evil is present with me. For I delight in the law of God after the inward man: But I see another law in my members, warring against the law of my mind, and bringing me into captivity to the law of sin which is in my members. O wretched man that I am! Who shall deliver me from the body of this death? I thank God through Jesus Christ our Lord. So then with the mind I serve the law of God; but with the flesh the law of sin. Only Jesus Christ can" Romans 7:15-25 (KJV)"

As we can plainly see, the problem is in dying to self. Self doesn't want to and will not willingly die. You have to crucify it. To crucify means to put to death by nailing or binding the hands and feet to a cross. Figurative it means to put to death by severe torture or persecution. The flesh gets no glory out of suffering and dying. It's one thing to be tortured or persecuted by someone else, but to crucify oneself is a painful task to undergo. This is the pain that flesh swiftly flee from.

Crucify: to defeat, torment, or victimize somebody in a thorough or cruel way; to put to death.

Jesus stated that, "If anyone who wants to be my follower must love Me far more than he does his own father, mother, wife, children, brothers or sister-yes, <u>even more than his own life</u>. Otherwise, he cannot be My disciple and no one can be My disciple who does not carry his own cross and follow Me." (Luke 14:26, 27 L B)

The cry of my flesh is a daily task that I face. It struggles to live while my spirit man fights to take its rightful position within me; to operate in the realm it was created to operate in. There's a war within! My flesh wars against my spirit. The sword of the Word is my weapon. I pierce my flesh to crucify my sinful natural. "Father" I cry, "Not my will, Thou will be done!"

I'm reminded of a story I once heard about an Indian who received Jesus Christ as his Savior. Each night he had the same dream that two dogs were fighting. One day he shared his dream with his chief. The chief asked, "Which dog would win the battle"? The Indian responded, "The one I fed the most".

The flesh is a way of thinking that leads to bad decisions which leads to failure. Failure doesn't come from being in the flesh or being out of control in your emotions but failure comes from making bad decisions and bad decisions come from being in the flesh and from letting your emotions rule over you.

Now don't get me wrong; but in reality, the enemy of our inheritance is not really the devil, but the flesh. The devil doesn't stop us from walking in the spirit and having what God wants us to have, it's our flesh. The flesh opposes the spirit and the spirit opposes the flesh. If you are not walking in your inheritance it is because you are not walking in the spirit.

The Bible doesn't say battle your flesh, but crucify your flesh. Romans 13:14 KJV "But put ye on the Lord Jesus Christ, and make not provision for the flesh, to fulfill the lusts thereof."

Galatians 5:24-25 (KJV) "And they that are Christ's have crucified the flesh with the affections and lusts. If we live in the Spirit, let us also walk in the Spirit." That means to walk in the power and by the leading of the Holy Spirit.

Failures always come from making bad decisions. Bad decisions always come from being led by your flesh.

Scripture also says that you have to take up your cross daily, not fight your flesh daily and that is because the flesh tries to bring itself back to life.

Luke 9:23 (KJV) "If any man will come after me, let him deny himself, and take up his cross daily, and follow me." What is your cross? Your cross is where your will, your desire, your thoughts are contrary to the thoughts, will and desire of God for your life. It is where your will and the will of God come into conflict and you have to do as Jesus when He walked as a man and prayed, "Father… not my will, but thine, be done" (Luke 22:42 KJV).

Why is this true? We can verify this with another scripture. Isaiah 55:8-9 (KJV) "For my thoughts are not your thoughts, neither are your ways my ways, saith the LORD. For as the heavens are higher than the earth, so are my ways higher than your ways, and my thoughts than your thoughts." So when we are following our ways, our thoughts, we are walking in the flesh because it is contrary to God's ways and God's thoughts which are given to us through His Word.

When a man is crucified, he dies. And when you die, you're dead. Therefore, those of us who belong to Jesus need to crucify the flesh so that we become dead to the flesh, dead to our passions, and dead to our desires. What is dead is the strings that attach us to sin that no longer bind us because they were cut loosed and destroyed by the Blood of Jesus and the Word of God. Galatians 2:20 (KJV) "I have been crucified with Christ and I no longer live, but Christ lives in me. The life I live in the body, I live by faith in the Son of God, who loved me and gave himself for me."

You Called?

Everything that happened to you in life, beginning with your childhood, is your path to destiny that has been designed by God for you. The call of my name upon my father's lips was in my path to destiny. I was purposely called. It taught me how to answer the many calls of God. Call is a common word, used in both the Old and New Testaments. We use it each day in a very common matter. Word Book states that "call" is to "say, especially in a loud voice by commanding or asking one to come." But as with many other common terms, Scripture often lifts "call" beyond the commonplace. When call is used in describing our relationship with the Father this simple word and the ideas it expresses has special significance.

> ### When God calls it indicates you are
> ### not where He wants you.

In most cases, the common Hebrew word "qara", means "to call". It is found meaning "to call on someone or something to bear witness." However, the root word "qara' suggest that it is "to utterance of a specific sound or message." When call involves a message, the one who receives it is "expected" to respond to the message.

When my father called me with the message, "Get up and light the heater", he expected me to respond to his call with obedience. When Father God calls, He too expects a response of obedience. It is also important to note that when God calls it indicates that you are not where

He wants you. When you are where God wants you He doesn't have to call, He just talks.

In my path to destiny I have discovered that God always wants me near, and He understood previous to time what it would take for me to get there. There in my path He placed the discipline of my father to teach me how to respond to His call.

Close Enough to Hear

Are you close enough to hear the sound of God's voice? Close enough to smell the fragrance of His Spirit. Close enough to hear the sound of His whisper? It is a sound that goes through you, a pure vibration that hits your ears and keeps going into the very core of your being; the sound of His voice. It is a humbling experience to be close enough to hear His voice. It is a close connection to God that allows you to erase any sense of time. The sound of God's voice is a wake-up call to open your ears and heart to His sound; the voice of creation. The sound of God's voice is like a voice that is still and silent and piercing at the same time. It will awaken the soul to self-examination.

I can recall the night when I heard the sound of God's voice. I had a vision that God was calling me. His voice was in a writing form of words on an index card. For some strange reason I ran from His voice on the card, like I ran from my father's voice. I saddled a horse in hope of out running it. It appeared that I was winning as I separated myself further and further from the card.

All of a sudden the letters of the card began to leave the card like an arrow being released from a bow. I could see the letters coming as they overtook me. Right into my very being, deep inside my soul they pierced. The letters spoke as they entered my soul. The sound of His voice pierced my being as He spoke to me saying, "Treat My ministry like a man of God"! From the sound of God's voice I knew the expression that was displayed upon His face. It was an expression of firmness; I respond today to that sound.

To Obey or not to Obey

Why is it so hard to obey? Is it because, "stolen waters are sweet, and bread eaten in secret is pleasant?" (Proverbs 9:17 KJV) Christ recognized that sometimes "the spirit indeed is willing, but the flesh is weak." (Matthew 26:41 KJV) James said that in many things we all stumble. It may be that our pride will not permit us to let go of our own control to submit to Him. Or do we fear being criticized as being weak? In the case of Adam and Eve they had more confidence in Satan's lie than they had in God. Often that which the world offers appears to be a much better deal than what one can see as the consequence of obeying God.

King Saul was commanded to destroy all of the herds of the enemy, but he couldn't see the point in getting rid of all that valuable livestock, so he overruled the command of God, and lost his kingdom and his life.

The one thing that we must realize is that man was created with a "will". A will is the power to choose to do or not to do. The word obey itself means to follow the orders by yielding to the control of something or person. Therefore, in order to obey one has to give up their will-power to choose and come under the control of another.

Stolen waters are sweet, and bread eaten in secret is pleasant

The Bible states that, "Know ye not that to whom ye yield yourselves servants to obey, his servants ye are to whom ye obey." Romans 6:16 (KJV). When you obey you become a servant to the one you yield to obey. Servant holds the same meaning as slave does, which means ownership. Man doesn't want to belong to anyone. He was not created to belong to. Man was created to be a part of. He was created to work "with" God and have fellowship "with" Him while being in partnership with Him. Man was created to rule with God. He is a ruler!

To yield is to give up ownership and to submit to. Remember, submission is not a creative performance, it is a learned performance. One has to learn to submit to the call of God. Your spirit and mind have to be trained to submit. Even as a child is trained to obey and to submit to their natural parents, so it is in the spirit realm with your heavenly Father.

To submit is to voluntarily put yourself in a position to be used by someone else. Even in responding to the call of God you voluntarily put yourself in a position to be used by God. Most of us think of being used by God is laying hands on sick people to be healed or speak a word into someone life; however, that's not so.

To be "used" is to be in a situation where you do all the suffering, go through all the hardship, while someone else reap the benefit; even as it was for me in lighting the family's heater. I had to of my own accord be used. I had to get out of a warm bed. I had to walk across a cold frozen floor. I had to bear the burden of the bitter cold, in order to light a heater that would bring pleasure to my father. I had to die that others may live. The problem was not in the lighting of the heater. The problem was doing it when he wanted and not when I wanted to. It would have been okay if I could have done it when I wanted to do it. The pain is in the dying, by coming under the control of another. Self does not want to submit!

Death: the condition or quality of being dead; the ending of all vital functions or processes in an organism or cell

Man, from the beginning was not created to die. I know this may be shocking to you but man was created to live and to live forever. He was created to have fellowship, be in partnership with, and to live with God forever. Man was not created to experience death. To die was never to be. To be a servant was never to be his task. He was created for Sonship, not servanthood. He was also created to obey. Obedience was not a task it was a lifestyle. He lived to obey. He was created to act in response to the voice of God. God's voice was the only voice he knew. Man was deceived by a voice he knew not.

Disobedience was a learned behavior for man. It's for this reason he ran from the voice and call of God, experiencing that which God never intended for him to experience. When God called him by name, "Adam"! He hid himself for he was naked. God asked him, "How do you know that you are naked? Have you done that which you were created not to do?" Adam sinned. Because of it he died. He was never created to die. Dying was a learned behavior for man.

Calling By Name

"You are no longer to call her Sari," God told Abraham Gen.17: 15 (KJV). Abraham's wife name was changed to "Sarah", meaning "princess". The naming and renaming of things, places, and persons is often seen in the Bible. For the Hebrews a name was more than a label. A name was an identifier, expressing significant information about the characteristic of the thing or person named. Nabal means "fool" and the man Nabal was a fool (1 Samuel 25:25 KJV). Abram means "father" and despite his age and childless state, he accepted the name change ordained by God; Abraham, "high father," or "father of a multitude" (Gen 17:5 KJV). Jesus means "Deliverer "for He shall save His people from their sin." (Matt 1:21 KJV)

Street Names

From the street I earned the name Wolf man, meaning a wild, long hair, beard wearing, and midnight wandering drug user. I was one that slept during the day and roamed during the wee hours of the night seeking a victim to rob or a purse to snatch. My street name expressed my characteristics as a drug user. Once becoming a believer the Holy Spirit directed me to stop people from calling me "Wolf man". Wolf man died the moment I received Christ as my Lord and Savior.

Your spirit lives in your name.

When you use your street name as becoming a believer, unbeknown to you, you are feeding the nature of the old man. By "nature" we mean you are feeding the personality of the old man. The personality is in the make-up and ways of the old man. He feeds on his name because his name keeps his character and personality alive.

There are spirits, characters and personalities that come with names. Spirits live in their names even as Jesus lives in his name. Jesus said that where two or three are gathered together in His name, there He would be in the midst of them. His existing would be in His name. In the physical, Jesus has returned to the right hand of power with the Father; however, His existing here on earth is in His name. When the name "Jesus" is spoken everything listens.

I recall once when we were riding to a revival service. I was driving and the back tire came off the van. My sisters was shouting, "Daddy, daddy!" Someone yelled my name, "Milton!" I was about to lose control of the van when I heard my mother shout, "Jesus!" All of a sudden that van came to a complete stop. The name Jesus put Him in our midst and He took control of the situation.

What's behind your name? From where did it come? Who told you that your name was Bunkum, Flick, Pistol Pete, Scarface, Mac, Timpo, Skeet, Hambone, Telee, Redbone or Cookie?

When you hear the voice of the Heavenly Father calling your name, the key is, respond to His calling. Even as the Lord called the name of Adam and he hid himself, so it will be to those who disobey the order of God. You are destined to be called and the greatest battle you will ever fight in life is the dying of one's self; to place yourself on the cross of death, dying by giving up your life in response to God, where your will no longer will be your own, but that of another. Not my will Thy will be done.

Trust has to become your best friend for now it is He upon whom you depend. Obedience is now a lifestyle for you to live by obeying His calling. His voice will become the common sound that you will hear in your ears for He shall call your name. When He does call and He will, remember to always respond to His voice. Your answer should always be, "Yes Lord."

Jesus lives and exists in His Name.

A Prophetic Word: Ye, I say unto you and be it known unto you that your name shall no longer be called Scar face or that of the world, because of an incident that happened in your past. You shall be called the Child of God! The very nature of your name shall be expressed when you are called. The ways, personalities, nature and character of your name shall be expressed as the Child of God! Your name shall be known in the port holes of hell said the Lord. Yea, even demons shall flee at the call of thy name. Thy name shall be "Child of God!" For the Lord has said, "I have called you by name; you are mine." (Isa 43:1 KJV). The Lord created, formed and redeemed you and has sealed the relationship by calling you His Child. God has claimed you as His own and approves His sovereign care over you.

CHAPTER VI

Sound Of Destiny

Revelation 21:4 (KJV) "And God shall wipe away all tears from their eyes; and there shall be no more death, neither sorrow, nor crying, neither shall there be any more pain: for the former things are passed away.

Ouch! That hurt. How many times have you heard that expression or even said it? Ouch! Ouch is an exclamation, expressing sudden pain. It's really more of a sound than it is a word. To be truthful about it, there's really not any word or words that can do justice in expressing destiny sound. Ouch is more of a sound that is expressed or associated with the beginning of a small pain. Have you ever noticed that no one had to teach you how to express the pain of destiny? No one taught you to say ouch. Where did it come? How does a child know to say ouch when pain is applied?

Ouch is the initial created sound of destiny.

Ouch is an expression from man's soul realm. It is the birthing forth of a seed that was planted in man's soul through the fall of man. Ouch is an expression that says pain has been born. When there's an enormous amount of pain, it is expressed more in a shout, scream or a yell that goes beyond the sound of words. That sound becomes an expression. That expression becomes the intense forceful sound of destiny. That sound is an expression that destiny is in progress. It's like the groan of a mother being expressed through the birthing of her child.

Mental pain is expressed more in deep moans than it is in an ouch. Moaning is a feeling or an expression of sorrow or grief made by a sound or utterance in a very sorrowful manner. Moaning is also a sound that expresses the initiate birthing forth of destiny. Mental pain can become so intense sometimes until you have to express it in a loud shout, a yell or scream. Many times I have had to drive away from everyone and just cry out with a loud shout, trying to relieve the pain from within. We all have or will experience this feeling in life.

Pain is a sign of life.

As stated earlier, of all the things I have experienced in life, there's nothing to compare to that of pain. There's a mystery about this strange impression that we all deal with. There is nothing about it that feels good, as a matter of fact there's no good word that is associated with it. Yet, in some strange way pain is good for us. How can anything that feels so bad be good for you? What is this strange impression? From where did it come? What's the purpose of it?

Mr. Webster states that pain is a feeling of being hurt or a feeling of suffering. Pain is also said to be mental suffering, grief or sorrow. In the Wordbook definition of pain it states said that hurt and suffering is the beginning process of birthing forth destiny. What's good about suffering or hurting? We do everything within our power to stop or avoid it. We run from it. Like a rabbit running from the mouth of a hungry hound dog, we flee from the presence of pain; yet, unbeknown to us, it is that force that causes us to run toward destiny in one way or another.

Our bodies deal with the pains of sickness, injuries and physical abuse while within our souls we deal with the pain of sorrow, grief, loneliness, disappointment and misunderstanding. Yes, pain is something that we all deal with. Life is not void of it! As a matter of fact there can be no life without pain.

Pain is an unpleasant feeling and emotional experience that is normally associated with hurts. Feeling is the act or condition of one that feels. It is the sense of touch; a sense of being connected to. By feeling we can feel what's hot or cold, soft or hard. We experience happiness and sadness, life and death through feeling. It's feelings that cause you to experience. Feeling is the connecting force that allows us to experience this great mystery of pain. Remove the feeling and there would be no pain. Removing or avoiding the source or sources of the situation that produces hurt can reduce or move destiny.

Feeling is also an emotion; a strong feeling of any kind. Joy, hate, sorrow and grief are feelings. Feeling or emotion is a pleasant or painful mental state produced in a person in reaction to a stimulus of some kind. Feeling is the general word while emotion is what moves feelings. If there were no feelings we would have no pains.

God can take the hurt out of the pain.

I was reading some material on a young boy whose body didn't have the sense of feeling. He would cut himself and be unaware of it. His limbs had been broken several times and the heel of his right foot was worn to the bone from stopping his bike with it. Infection set in his body and the boy died. Therefore, I must say, as bad as it may hurt, it's a blessing to feel pain. Persons who are born without the ability to feel pain or develop such an inability are at great risk of the consequences of unrecognized hurts.

Pain is a sign of life. Pain is a sign that you are connected to destiny. A friend of mine had an accident that caused injury to his spinal cord. He lost feeling in his upper body. His nerves were disconnected from his spinal cord. They were not in touch with one another. After a period of time, feeling of pain began in his upper body. That pain was a sign that his nerves were connecting again. Does it feel good? No! Is it good? Yes! Daily he's experiencing the feeling of pain. By doing so he's also experiencing the birthing forth of health. The phrase no pain, no gain is at work in his life.

Pain and suffering have been themes for many as a mystery, however, when we enter a time of suffering, all the wisest speculations of this mystery seems empty and meaningless. We simply hurt and want release. We struggle to cope with our pains. Sometimes even when we look to Scriptures to find a Word on pain that will heal or bring release, it seems that we find little hope. As a matter of fact, Scriptures have no magic remedy that will remove pain and suffering from among us. Suffering is a part of life, thanks to Adam.

As long as we are in this sinful world, we will have to deal with pain. However, there is a perspective on suffering that if we adopt by faith, God can take the hurt out of the pain. God doesn't remove the pain; He just takes the feeling of hurt from the pain. Many will ask you, "How are you dealing with it"? The answer would be, "God has taken the hurt out of it."

Pain is a seed that has been planted.

The thing that amazes me the most about pain is the fact that it is an experience that affects us from within. It affects the soul realm of man. It can cause fear and doubt when the patterns of one's lives are shaken by it. You will seek to find answers to, "Why am I suffering? What did I do to cause or deserve this?" These are the questions that Job asked. In many cases pain does not come because of something you've done but because of something someone else has done. From whatever source it may come, pain will push you into your destiny.

Who Broke The Law?

Pain is the violation of the law. Pain was first introduced to the human race after the fall of man. Previous to this there was no pain. Pain is the result of breaking the law. The origin of pain was in the Garden of Eden. (Genesis 3:16, 17 KJV) "To the woman He said, I will greatly increase your pains in childbearing; with pain you will give birth to children. Your desire will be for your husband, and he will rule over you. To Adam He said, Because you listened to your wife and ate from the tree about which

I commanded you, 'You must not eat of it,' cursed is the ground because of you; through painful toil you will eat of it all the days of your life."

Therefore, pain is the result of breaking God's law. The breaking of God's law is sin. (1 John 3:4 KJ "Whosoever committeth sin transgresses also the law: for sin is the transgression of the law." Pain is the punishment that God placed upon Adam and Eve for sin. The law was "don't eat of the tree of the knowledge of good and evil." (Gen 2:17 KJV)

The moment Adam sinned; he stopped operating in the realm that he was created to operate. He was created to operate in the realm of obedience and righteousness. He was like God; as a matter of fact he was a god. He was made in the image and likeness of his father. The world was perfect as he operated in that realm. There was no sickness, evil, pain, sorrow, hurts or death. These things came about as the result of Adam's violation of God's law. Pain came from that violation.

From the day Adam sinned till now we all experience the consequence of that sin. Pain is a constant reminder of sin's origin. The pain and suffering of the human condition are an outcome and a reminder of man's broken relationship with God. Pain is linked not only with an individual choice but also with the sinful condition of Adam. It is a seed that was planted long ago. Despite all our pain, there's something good about it. Pain will one day bring new life. It is God's overall plan to bring you into your destiny of new life.

Pain is a sign that new life is coming forth.

The origin of pain is not just for punishment. It's not just a punishment for wrongdoing. It's a prick that will make you do what you don't want to do. It is this same principle that we apply today. When our child violates the rule or rules we have set, we punish them by inflecting pain in some form. Be it in a spanking or withholding certain privileges from them.

The objective of punishment is to cause discomfort. Through the discomfort of pain, destiny will be birthed. Understanding now that the overall view and purpose for the discomfort is to force the child or person, again I say 'force' the person to do what they wouldn't otherwise do on their own. There's a place where you are trying to get the child. It is called a place of obedience, the place where the child was created to operate in from the beginning of time. It is a place of destiny.

Pain can cause you to do that which you don't want to do. It can make a strong man break like shadow glass. It can make tears fall from the eyes of superman. It can make you stay awake all night while your body cries out for sleep. Pain can make you go against your will, causing you to obey when you want to do otherwise. Yes, pain is a breaker. It can cause the strongest of men to breakdown like a double barrel shotgun, and that's a fact.

It's a Fact

Fact is something known to be true: something that can be shown to be true, to exist, or to have happened. In layman's terms fact is the truth or reality of something that actually exists or happens. It's a fact that we are in this world. We exist. It's a fact that we are of a particular race. As for me I'm an African American. That's a fact. It's of a fact that you are either a male or female person. It is also a fact that you had nothing to do with being here, your race, or your gender. It was your entire mother's and father's doing. They did the do and you came as a result of their pleasure. That's a fact.

It's a fact that since I am here, I will one day leave here; no one stays forever. It doesn't matter how badly we desire to stay, all must leave. That's a fact. It's a fact that between coming and leaving here there's a space and period that we call life. It's a fact that in life you will be dealt a hand to play that you had nothing to do with. The reason being is because God is the dealer, you are the receiver.

Allow me to explain that there's nothing that's happening in your life that God is not aware of. I know it may be hard for you to understand this concept especially if what's happening is bad. No doubt Job felt the same way, while living a godly and faithful life for God and Satan destroyed all he had. In reading the story of Job, Satan could do nothing to Job except God released him to do so.

The hand that was dealt to Job was sent by God. God told Satan what he could and couldn't do. The devil may have brought it but God sent it because God is in control. In reading the last chapter of Job, he was blessed with twice as much as he had in the beginning. God used the devil to bless Job to reach his destiny. A destiny of blessing! It may have been a setup by Satan to destroy Job; howbeit, Satan's setup was inside of God's setup to bless Job with a destiny of blessings. God has a destiny of blessings for you.

Yes, the sound and expression of pain was heard through the scream of Job's voice. He cursed the day he was born. Broken skin covered his entire body. All of his children were dead and everything he had was gone. Even his closest friends saw him as one that had sinned greatly. Job had no idea as to what God's purpose was for his life as he endured the pains of destiny. Nevertheless, Job played the hand that God dealt him.

What will you do with the hand you've been dealt? You have two choices. You can fold your hand, based on the fact that you had nothing to do with it, or you can play the hand. The choice is yours. Allow me to serve notice that in playing your hand, it doesn't always mean you'll win the game, it simply means that you must do the best with what you've been dealt. Life dealt it, but you'll make the best of it because your hand will lead you to your expected end!

It's a fact that in the game of life there are at least two things you will deal with; pain and fear. It is also a fact that pain brought you here. Upon entering this world your mother went through pain, and after entering this world your first experience was pain. You entered this world in an upside down position not breathing. The doctor took you by the heel in this up-side-down position and smacked you on your bottom and pain came. It's bad enough coming here in an up-side-down position without the pain. But pain is good for you.

Pain is a sign of life. Anything that's dead can't feel pain. Through the pain, from the smack on your bottom, you began to breath. Your body went through a moment of shock. Through that shocking experience your first emotion was birth; the birth of destiny. Destiny caused you to release the cry of life. Crying caused you to breathe. Yes, pain is good for you even when it's not good to you.

Pain forced you to do what you would not have done on your own. It pushed you from the comfort of your mother's womb. Pain forced you into your destiny of life. Pain is like that; it will make you do what you never dreamed you would or could do. It will make you face your greatest fears of stepping outside of your comfort zone into your destiny of life. God uses everything in your life to get you to your destiny. There is a sound being heard, it's the sound of destiny.

CHAPTER VII

The Voice in My Tears

"He that sows in tears shall reap in joy. He that goeth forth and weepeth, bearing precious seed, shall doubtless come again with rejoicing, bringing his sheaves with him." (Psalm 126:5, 6 KJV)

Why do we cry? Is it because we have stubbed our toe or shut the door upon our finger? What does a tear say? The word "say" in this term is to convey something over and above the uttering or words or exterior sound by being expressed in an appearance. The most natural reason we cry, as in shedding tears, is because of an emotional expression that has taken place in the soul realm; be it an expression of sadness, happiness, grieving, or simply being upset.

Tears express man's thoughts and emotions. Tears are the silent voice of your soul. Tears are not water that runs from your eyes from cutting an onion. Tears are expressions being voiced. Though all tears look alike, there are different tears for different emotions and thoughts. In every emotional tear there's a voice crying out. The window of your soul is displaying visibly the hidden thoughts of the soul.

One amazing discovery that I have found is that God has placed within every tear an aid to help a person deal with emotional problems. There's healing in your tears. This finding helps me understand the expression, "To cry it out helps a person feel better." Have you noticed that after crying, you actually do feel better, both physically and mentally, and you feel worse by suppressing your tears. I believe that stress, worrying and sad-induced tears actually bring healing to the mind and body.

Tears are visible thoughts and emotions of the soul.

I once read that in a study volunteers were led to cry first from watching sad movies, and then from freshly cut onions. It was found that the tears from the movies, called emotional tears, contained far more toxins. Based upon this study it was concluded that crying is a process which removes toxic substances that normally build up during emotional stress. What a wonderful and amazing God to place such an amazing element in man.

It was also discovered that suppressing tears increases stress levels, and contribute to diseases such as high blood pressure, heart problems and ulcers. No wonder the Word states that a merry heart is good like medicine. There's healing in tears.

Destiny Cry

The Psalm states that he that sows in sorrow shall reap in joy. I can recall witnessing such an event with my family. It was a bitter cold winter morning. The family was about performing daily duties while mom and dad were down town shopping. The old family heater was lit and warmth filled the room. My sisters were asleep in their room while I was in the family room cutting my brothers' hair. We were too poor to go to the barbershop so I was the family's barber.

From her cold room, my youngest sister came dashing toward the open heater to warm her small thin cold body. No doubt laugher filled the room as her body shook from the bitter cold. As she stood close to the space heater, her nightgown exploded in fire and went up in flames.

The cry of her voice could be heard throughout the house as she ran about the room screaming, yelling and shouting, "help me, please, help me!" Not knowing what to do, I ran to her aid, ripping the flaming clothes from her body with my bare hands, receiving second degree burns. The pain was intense as I fought to free her. The house was filled with noise as my siblings ran through the house yelling and screaming for help. Granddaddy raced from the back room yelling, "Get some water; please get some water!" Confusion was everywhere!

The front door opened and my sister ran outside. I fought with all my might to stop her. The flames covered her entire body. The smell of burning flesh filled my nostrils. I was losing the battle and I knew it. She yelled, "Please, help me Milton, please help me!" I pushed her to the ground trying to roll her. Tears filled my eyes as the shout of her voice pierced my very being. Within my tears was the voice of my soul crying out. It was the cry of destiny, filled with sorrow and pain.

What does a small boy do in such a horrific situation? Little did I know that this was a predetermined event that was in God's plan, but not in His will. Destiny was being fulfilled. It was more than I could handle. The saving of her life was in my hands. She asked for help but there was none I could give. Destiny cried out through the voice of my tears. My inner thoughts were expressed as they fell freely down my cheeks. One minute seemed to have been an eternity. Time appeared to stand still as I searched for the answer. What could stop this tragedy? Nothing, destiny will be fulfilled and I was a part of it.

At the moment the only thing I knew to do was what I saw and heard my mother do many times as a child. When life's burdens became unbearable for her and time became hard, she would always look up and say, "Lord help me." With everything within me, I lifted my head to the Hill from which cometh my help and shouted from my inner being, "Lord help me!"

Psalm 91:1-6 (KJV) "He that dwelleth in the secret place of the most High shall abide under the shadow of the Almighty. I will say of the Lord, He is my refuge and my fortress: my God; in him will I trust. Surely he shall deliver thee from the snare of the fowler, and from the noisome pestilence. He shall cover thee with his feathers, and under his wings shalt thou trust: his truth shall be thy shield and buckler. Thou shalt not be afraid for the terror by night; nor for the arrow that flieth by day; Nor for the pestilence that walketh in darkness; nor for the destruction that wasteth at noonday."

A Bird or a Plane?

From the corner of my right eye, out of nowhere, I could see him coming. Faster than a lightning flash he suddenly appeared. An angel! From where did he come? From God is all I know. I stood in amazement as I watched him remove his coat from his body and wrapped it quickly around my sister. The fire was out. Thank God! As he removed his coat from her burned thin body, what was left of her burned nightgown and flesh lined the inside of it. Very carefully he folded it, placed it upon his forearm and walked away without saying one word.

My sister laid on the ground. She was weak and shaking uncontrollable. Her eyes were wide open; her voice was weak as she continued to ask me for help. She could still feel the pain from the fire. The pain was intense. Closely to my body I held her, trying to comfort her as destiny cried out. The ambulance came and took her through the downtown area to the nearby hospital. Little did my parents know that the ambulance that passed by them, as they shopped, carried their own little girl.

The doctors examined her condition. She had received third degree burns over eighty percent of her body. Her ears were burned halfway off. The tip of her nose was burned off. Her upper legs, upper body, arms and hands were severely burned. Even her intestines were burned. After examining her the doctor told the head nurse that she was not going to live. They pushed her into a room, put a tent over her body and gave her medicine to help relieve the pain while awaiting her death.

Sadness filled the house of the Adams. Tears of sorrow were expressed upon each face. Every tear expressed the inter pain of each family member. We all did what we could to comfort each other with a kiss, a hug, or a soft-spoken word. Mom spent days and nights at the bedside of her dying daughter. Dad went about trying to care for the family, burning bread and heating leftovers to feed us. I did my part by keeping the guys up on the latest hairstyle and preparing my sisters' hair for school each morning. We all worked together to get through each day.

My father would go to the hospital each day to visit, bringing comfort to his hurting depressed wife. One Saturday morning dad was lying across the bed trying to rest from the overbearing burden of life's destiny. The phone rang. The cry of my mother's voice screamed in a rage saying,

"Hurry, hurry! The baby is dying! If you want to see her before she dies, hurry to the hospital!"

The call of my name was once again upon my father's voice. It was a sound of turmoil. Milton! Again I responded to his call by running to his side. The look upon his face told me everything. Tears filled his eyes. Without saying a word I could hear the voice of his tears cried out for help. He looked me in my face with such desperation. "Go and tell the saints to pray", he said, "The baby is dying!"

I ran as fast as I could through the streets of Greenwood, Mississippi. Going from door to door crying and asking people to pray. It matter not what color they were, black, brown, yellow, orange, blue, green, red or white. The only thing that mattered was my baby sister; she was dying and we were in need of prayer.

My father rushed to give support to my mother. As he entered the doors of the hospital he found mom pacing back and forth, up and down the hospital hallway. The cry of destiny rang from her voice. "My baby, my baby, my baby," she screamed! Destiny's cry could be heard throughout the hospital as my mother cried for mercy. Everyone knew the sound. Her child was dying.

The doctors walked out of her room. They told my parents there was nothing more that could be done. My baby sister died. My father walked into her room. Her head had dropped in the lock of her shoulder. Foam ran down the side of her mouth. Life departed her body. Destiny cried.

Sorrow filled the very soul of my father's being. Intense pain pierced his heart. Tears again ran unstoppable down his cheeks as he walked over to a window to pray. What do you say? How do you pray in this type of situation? The Holy Spirit instructed my father to call Miracle Valley and ask the A. A. Allen prayer team to pray.

In the mist of all the pain, sorrow, grief, and hurt God began to speak to my father. God can use your pain to speak to you. As my father stood in the window praying for his daughter, there in the bed next to his child was another mother's child dying also. He felt nothing for her because he wasn't connected to her. God used this moment of sorrow to cause my father to pay attention to others who were also in need of prayer. Prayer was offered for both of them.

When "LIFE" enters a room death has to go.

Jesus Christ came walking into that hospital room with healing in His wings. When Life enters a room, death has to leave. Jesus touched my sister with His finger of life and restored life into her dead body. Not only did Jesus touch her body He also touched the child that was in bed next to her. Health and healing came to their rescue. His name is Jesus. A calm sleep came on my sister as doctors rushed in to witness this miracle of destiny.

My little sister woke up the next morning with a smile upon her face. Mom had gone home to get rest. My Aunt Rosie, who spent the night, asked my sister could she sing a song. She opened her mouth and sung, "I Got Just What I Wanted From The Lord!" God raised Darlene from that hospital's deathbed and restored life to her. Destiny was fulfilled. Tears that were sown in sorrow were now being reaped in joy. What a mighty God we serve, He showed up on time.

He'll Show Up

How do you get God to show up in your life when things are bad and you need Him? Is it through tears of sorrow and a broken soul? Well let me ask you, "Have you ever cried in tears and no answer came"? Tears don't move God to act. Tears releases stress and bring healing and glory to the one crying. It is praises that brings glory to God. He always shows up to receive His glory. The Bible states in Psalm 50:23 KJV "Whoso offereth praise glorifieth Me: and to him that ordereth his conversation aright will I show the salvation of God". God will always show up in His Praises. Praise Him! Tears don't move God, but praises does! The Word says that the LORD dwells in the praises of His people. "But thou art holy, O thou that inhabitest the praises of Israel" Psalm 22:3 (KJV). When you are going through, praise Him and He will show up.

However, one must also remember that God doesn't always show up to change the situation. He may just show up in order to give you the strength you need to endure the situation as He did with me when facing the situation with my sister. God is not so concerned about always changing the situation as He is about changing you. Changing you will enable you to deal with the situation and reach your expected end.

The problems you face will either defeat you or develop you, depending on how you respond to them. Unfortunately most people fail to see how God wants to use problems for good in their lives. They react foolishly and resent their problems rather than pausing to consider what benefit they might bring.

Believe it or not God uses problems to direct you. Sometimes God has to light a fire under you to get you moving. Problems often point us in a new direction and motivate us to change. Is God trying to get your attention? No, He's not "trying", He is! "Sometimes it takes a painful situation to make us change our ways." (Proverbs 20:30 KJV) states that, "Blows that hurt cleanse away evil, as do stripes the inner depths of the heart."

At the heart of this verse is the message that punishment needs to be harsh or painful enough to make a difference in behavior. (Hebrews 12:11 KJV) "Now no chastening seems to be joyful for the present, but painful; nevertheless, afterward it yields the peaceable fruit of righteousness to those who have been trained by it."

When a child is punished for, let's say, rebellion, in a way that does not get his attention, so to speak, he often decides, "Well, if that's all that I earned then it was worth it!" While the principle shouldn't push us to abuse; however, it should remind us to make certain that our discipline causes a strong enough impression on a child's mind so as to truly motivate him differently the next time the same temptation presents itself.

There are times when God will show up and we miss Him. The reason is because sometimes He doesn't appear or operates in the fashion we desire or expect of Him. Sometimes He doesn't look like God and if we are not careful we will call God's work the devil. Here's the point. God is at work in your life even when you do not recognize it. But it's much easier and profitable when you cooperate with him and praise Him in the midst of it.

Praise Him With One Accord.

Whatever you are going through, praise God with every part of you! Praise God with your whole mind, spirit and body. Bring the total you into a one accord of praise. Tongues are your spirit praising God. Tears are an expression of your soul and thoughts giving praise. Hand clapping, foot stumping are expressions of the body giving God praise. Bring the total you into a harmony of praise and God will always show up.

Tongues are your spirit praising God. Tears are an expression of your soul and thoughts giving praise.

When Solomon finished building the temple and the praisers began to praise God in harmony, God showed up. "It came even to pass, as the trumpeters and singers were as **one**, to make **one sound** to be heard in praising and thanking the LORD; and when they lifted up their voice with the trumpets and cymbals and instruments of musick, and praised the LORD, saying, For he is good; for his mercy endureth for ever: that then the house was filled with a cloud, even the house of the LORD; So that the priests could not stand to minister by reason of the cloud: for the glory of the LORD had filled the house of God." (II Chronicles 5:13-14 KJV).

When Jehoshaphat, the king of Judah, dwelt in Jerusalem, the enemy surrounded and outnumbered him. However, God send a Word by His prophet. After the prophet encouraged him, he sent the choir out before the army to praise God and God showed up. "And when he had consulted with the people, he appointed singers unto the LORD, and that should praise the beauty of holiness, as they went out before the army, and to say, Praise the LORD; for his mercy endureth forever. And when they began to sing and to praise, the LORD set ambushments against the children of Ammon, Moab, and mount Seir, which were come against Judah; and they were smitten." (II Chronicles 20:21-22 KJV).

You may be in the situation because the enemy has come up against you and surrounded you. However, God will show up when you praise Him. Your sorrow will be made to be joy! You may be in the situation because you have been running from God. However, when you praise God in the middle of the situation, God will show up to deliver you.

When praises goes up, blessing comes down!

In 1999, my father had a heart attack and had to undergo a surgical procedure to repair six blockages in his heart. Doctors did all they could do to save him. My father died. The pain of death bore heavily upon each heart. Family members from all over came together and began to just give God praise. We praise Him in harmony and with every part of our being. We praised Him with our tears of sorrow. We praised Him with our tongues. We praised Him with our hands and bodies. We praised Him with everything we had! While we were praising God at home a miracle was taking place in the hospital. God gave life back to my father! Joy was given for sorrow!

My tears are words that my heart can't express.
They are the silent voice of my inner-being.

An Attitude of Praise

One of the most important steps you can take toward achieving your greatest potential in life is to learn to observe your attitude of praise and its impact on your relationships with God.

It's always good to have a good attitude in a bad situation; however, it's always better to have an attitude of praise in every situation. We must praise God regardless of the situation. Your victory is in your praise. When Paul and Silas, because of their preaching the gospel, were thrown into prison, in isolation, and with their feet in stock, they sang praises to God and God showed up.

"And at midnight Paul and Silas prayed, and sang praises unto God: and the prisoners heard them. And suddenly there was a great earthquake, so that the foundations of the prison were shaken: and immediately all the doors were opened, and every one's bands were loosed." (Acts16:25 KJV).

You may be in a situation because of unjust persecution. However, when you praise God in the situation, God will come through for you. It doesn't matter how bad your situation is, if you will praise God in the midst of that situation, He will always show up on the scene and your tears sown in sorrow will be reaped in joy.

CHAPTER VIII

Your Door to an Expected End

(Jeremiah 29:11KJV) "For I know the thoughts that I think toward you, saith the LORD, thoughts of peace, and not of evil, to give you an expected end".

I stood as I listened to the conversation of young men in the ministry. Their conversation was that of normal teenagers, talking about sports, clothes, school and girls. I asked one of the teenagers, "How are things with you and your girl?" He responded to me by saying, "Pastor, that's dead, we ain't got it going on like that no more. We ain't connected like that." (I try to keep up with the style of the youth without being caught up in unworldly fashion and words). What did he mean when he said, "That's dead, and we ain't got it going on like that no more and we ain't connected like that?" In simple terms he meant, "We are separated." That's dead means there's no life in the relationship, not connected.

Being alive is the result of being connected to life.

Life and Death

When there's no understanding of death, the word death itself appears frightening. Death has been pictured as a dreadful thing, being black, dark, cold, bitter and chilling. We run from it. No one seeks its face. What is it about death that people fear? Many say that it is the mystery of death that people fear. Whatever it is, people fear it.

What is this mysterious thing? From where did it come? Is it a natural thing? World Book states that death is the act or fact of dying; it is the ending of any form of life in people, animals, or plants. Death is the separator of a thing from its source. It comes to separate! Have you ever picked up the phone and found no dial tone? We say, "The phone is dead." The phone is dead because it's not connected to its source. Death separated it.

Upon this term of death I must say and shock some of you too, death can be the door to your destiny, your expected end. It all depends upon what death is separating you from. It is the pain of separation that people fear, the pain of not being connected anymore. On that same note there are many who welcome the coming of death; to be separated from the pains of a bad relationship, or the pains of sickness, sorrow and grief. Pain could cause you to welcome death.

In understanding that death is a separator, we can now better understand the nature of it by understanding what it comes to do. Death is the separator that separates a living thing from the source that gives it the ability to live in a particular stage, which includes the process of dying and the pain and suffering associated with decaying.

Death was first introduced into the universe after the sins of Adam and Eve. Prior to the Fall there was no death for man. Man only knew Life; live, eat, drink, have sex and be merry. God commanded man saying, "You must not eat from the tree of the knowledge of good and evil, for when you eat of it you will surely die" (Gen 3:6-7 KJV).

Adam and Eve ate of the tree and death was introduced to mankind. Death was the doorway that separated man from his eternal destiny and death is the door to bring man back into his eternal destiny, his expected end. To better understand what happens when death was introduced, we need to first have a clear picture of Life.

What is LIFE?

Life is to be alive, to live. Upon studying this term my spirit wasn't completelly satisfied with this definition. It did not bring fulfillment or closure to my spirit man. Life has to be more than being alive or to live; that's what life "does". Life causes one or something to be alive or live. When something is "alive" it has life. Alive is a state of existence or the principle of existence conceived by belonging to or being connected to life; therefore, alive or to live comes from being connected to life.

There first has to be Life "before" something or someone can live or be alive. There first has to be life in order for something to be connected to it. If something is "connected" that tells me that it has to be connected to something or someone. Being alive is the result of being connected to life. Life is therefore the source from which everything alive is connected. If it is alive it is connected to what gives it the ability to live. What is it that gives everything that's alive the ability to live? If we can find the answer to that question, we can discover what Life is.

Gen 1:1(KJV) tells us that, "In the beginning GOD created the heavens and the earth." It goes on to tell us that everything that was made came from Him and without Him there isn't nothing made that is made.

Life comes from the breath of God.

"And the Lord God formed man of the dust of the ground, and breathed into his nostrils the breath of life: and man became a living soul" (Gen 2:7 KJV).

(Job 27:3 KJV) "...as long as I have **life** within me, the **breath** of God in my nostrils."

God and Christ are the absolute source and cause of all life.

(John 1:4 KJV) "In Him (God) was life, and the life was the light of Man."

(John 5:26 KJV) "For as the Father hath life in Himself, so hath He given to the Son to have life in Himself."

As the Word has plainly stated, life comes from and is God. All things were dead or none existent until it was connected to God. There was nothing until it became connected to God! Adam was nothing but a dead corpse, from the dust or the earth, until God connected Adam to Himself by breathing the breath of Life in his nostrils; once that happened, the Bible said that Adam became a living soul. Adam was now connected to Life and began to live.

Not only did Adam become physically alive, he became spiritually and eternally alive. When God placed His seed (His life) inside of Adam's body, Adam became spiritually alive as the Son of God. He was born to live throughout eternity with God, having dominion over the earth as God's under-ruler. Earth was to be a visible manifestation of the invisible world of God. This was man's destiny.

Three things happened when Adam was born, (born means to come forth or brought into life). He was born physical, spiritual and eternal. Adam was connected to God in all three realms. Adam was connected physically by the breath of God being blown into his physical body and his body became alive. He was connected spiritually by having the seed of God in him, making him the Son of God, made in the image of God. Within the seed of life comes the personality of God. Adam was connected eternally by being connected to God to live forever as an eternal, spiritual being made in the likeness of God as a god, fulfilling his purpose and destiny.

Destiny for Righteousness

Righteousness is the power to stand in God's presence without sense of fear and condemnation. Adam was born for righteousness. Righteousness is man's destiny. He was born holy, saved, upright and pure. He was born the Son of God. Righteousness was the key that connected Adam with his Father. Righteousness gave Adam a legal right to live in the presence of God. As a matter of fact righteousness made Adam one with God and righteousness made him as God. As long as Adam operated in righteousness he was destined to be God's Son of Righteousness and to be a god.

You were created to be a god!

Even as it was with Adam, so is it with you. You were born again to operate in righteousness and have the power to stand in the presence of God without a sense of fear and condemnation. You are destined to be God's Child of Righteousness and a god. The Bible states, "Be not deceive, he that does righteousness **is** righteous even as He is Righteous (1 John 3:7 KJV).

When you operate in righteousness you become righteous like God. You becomes what God is; Righteous. Righteous is the act of doing right. Righteousness moves fear.

As a young boy growing under my father's authority, when I obeyed my father, I had no fear of standing in his presence. An act of disobedience birthed fear and because of unrighteousness you will hide from God's presence.

Destiny for Sonship

As we stated earlier, Adam was born for Sonship. God wanted a son to rule with Him. He was to be partner with God, operating in the same class with God. He was not GOD; however, he was a god. When the devil told Eve, "if you eat of the tree of the knowledge of good and evil you would become as gods" (Gen 3:5 KJV), she was already a god.

In order to be in the class with God, you had to be "like" God. "Like" is to be the same as; in nature, makeup and character. When something is like something, you cannot tell the difference between them. God is Spirit: Man is spirit. God is God. Man is a god. Let's look at it from this view. Everything produces after its kind. A dog begets a dog. A cat begets a cat. A horse begets a horse. A devil begets a devil. God begets gods.

Operating in Righteousness connects you to God.

Purpose to Reproduce Life

God could have spoken the entire human race into existence, however He chose not to. God made Adam and Eve fellow workers with Him in reproducing Life.

101

(Gen 1:28 KJV) "And God blessed them, and God said unto them, be fruitful, and multiply, and replenish the earth and subdue it."

Adam and Eve's greatest job was to give birth to God's children, eternal beings who would be like God. Life was in Adam because Adam was connected to Life. Adam's connection was through righteousness by obeying the commandments of God. Life comes through obedience. Obedience keeps you connected to God. As long as Adam obeyed God he operated in righteousness. That righteousness kept him in Life. That Life kept him alive.

Adam's life was in God. There is no life without Him. Adam and God was one in Spirit, union, and righteousness. Connection to God gives you life, for God is LIFE. Obedience is the connection key to life. Disobedience is the separator. Obey and live. Disobey and die. The moment Adam sinned death separated him from his destiny; therefore, death will be the door to bring him back to his destiny. Death separated and death would restore life.

The Faces of Deaths

Death wears more than one face. Death has three different faces. There are three different types of death. There is a natural death, spiritual death and eternal death. Three faces, one death.

Natural Death

Natural death is the face that we are most acquainted with. Natural death is the separation of the spirit and soul from the body. When a man die his body goes to the earth but his spirit and soul goes back to God from which he cometh. This death is a physical death. Adam's sin of disobedience brought the entrance of death into the life of man.

Spiritual Death

Spiritual death is a state of existence in a condition separated from God. Spiritual death is the first death that was introduced to man. God said to Adam, "The day you eat of the tree of the knowledge of good and evil you will surely die." (Gen 2:17 KJV) When Adam ate of the tree, the breaking of God's law came into being. That sin became the separator. Death was birthed through sin. There was no death until sin came. Adam became separated from God through sin.

One must understand what happened at the breaking of God's law. At the breaking of God's law, Adam became a "born again" being. "Born again" means to first die to your present life and to come into existence again to a new life that's totally different than the former. The Son of God died and the son of sin was born when Adam sinned. He was no longer the Son of Righteousness; he was now the son of sin. Adam's spirit became born again from life to death through a spiritual sexual intercourse with sin that produced a sinner. Adam cheated on God! He had relationship with sin and that act brought a new child into being; a sinner. This child was that of God's enemy, the devil, of whom He cast out of heaven. Because of this act God drove Adam from His presence.

Death was birth out of sin.

(Gen 3:23-24 KJV) "Therefore the Lord God sent him (Adam) forth from the Garden of Eden, to till the ground from whence he was taken. So He drove out the man..."

A two-fold thing took placed when Adam sinned. Two deaths came into being, spiritual and physical. Spiritual death manifested itself in the physical body of Adam. His body became mortal, meaning worldly. He was spiritually dead the moment he sinned but he did not die physically for 930 years. When God told Adam that the day he ate of the tree of the knowledge of good and evil he would surly die, God was speaking about spiritual death, not natural death.

Eternal Death
Eternal death is called the "second death" in the book of Revelation 20"11-15. This death is an eternal separation from God in a state of existence; however, forever separated from God's presence. This existence

will come about after the Great White Throne Judgment when God will separate the wicked from the believers. Now that's dead.

Man is the living link in life that binds the creation with God, by connecting heaven to earth.

THE BOOK OF ADAMS

CHAPTER IX

What Did I Do Wrong?

Proverbs 22:6 (KJV) "Train up a child in the way he should go: and when he is old, he will not depart from it."

The sun shined brightly as I sat waiting for my former wife to return to the car. Life had been good and we were about to have a nice lunch and enjoy the moment with our oldest son. The birds sang as they went about building nests on this early spring day.

The door of the house opened and there she stood in the doorway. Her body was dysfunctional as she tried to move toward me. Something was wrong! I ran to her side as she collapsed in my arms. She breathed heavily as she struggled to speak to me but no words would form upon her lips. "What's wrong", I shouted! Please talk to me!

Tears filled her eyes as she struggled to pull herself together. The expression on her face reflected the brokenness of a hurting heart. This brokenness would cause much more pain and dysfunction in our life. More than I ever dreamed.

My son had committed a crime and was being held in confinement facing twenty-five years. My heart hurt from the pain. I searched for answers but there were none. How could this be? I raised my son in church. I taught him the ways of the Lord. I am a pastor! I asked myself the question, "What did I do wrong?" So much pain! The pattern of my live was shaken and my expectation had failed.

How many of you are disappointed with the path and decision family members have made? Decisions that have shaped the path of your life that's totally different from the dreams and plans you desired? I want to encourage you by saying, "There's something good in the storm."

Yes, it was a dark day even while the sun shined so brightly on this early spring morning. Why me? What did I do wrong? This was the song I sang day after day. I have heard this song sang by many others as they search for answers, answers that never came.

Many times the pains of sorrow and grief will cause you to search for answers to unanswerable questions. Why did she or he leave me? Why was my child raped? Why much pain? Why the suffering? What did I do wrong? Many times you can experience pain not because you did wrong but because someone you are connected to did wrong. It's like reaping where you didn't sow.

The pain of the body is often bearable.
Not so is the pain of the heart.

However, it's your connection that causes you to feel the pain. The same situation could happen to someone else and you would never feel it. Allow me to say this, "Many times, as believers, we think that as being a child of God we are exempt from the pains of life". This is by far wrong. We are not exempt. As a matter of fact we are more of a target for the intense unpleasant physical and emotional distress experienced by somebody who is violently struck, injured, or ill.

Pain may be punishment directed by God at the wicked; suffering may also come to the innocent through the action of the wicked. As strange as it sounds, there are times that God will allow pain to come into our lives as it was with the prophet Hosea. God may at times use it as a tool to bring understanding to us.

God instructed Hosea to marry a woman that would be unfaithful to him. Through this relationship Hosea experienced the brokenness, grief and sorrow caused by an unfaithful wife. Why would God instruct a man to do such a thing? God wanted Hosea to feel and understand what He felt with Israel. His people was unfaithful to Him. God wanted Hosea to walk a mile with Him in His shoes. God wants you to walk a mile with Him in His shoes. You will never understand a person until you walk a mile in their shoes. When God uses pain, there's a purpose.

Job was a man that God called blameless and upright (Job 1:8); his long prosperity was suddenly transformed into tragedy. His wealth, family, the respect of his peers, and health were taken away in a single day. However, God was the link to Job's suffering.

Job's friend argued that some secret sin must have been the cause of his suffering. His pain was his punishment. I too can relate to Job. At the conviction of my son many pointed fingers at me and blamed me for the tragedy of my family. It was told to me that I wasn't doing right. I wasn't covering my family. It was because of some sin I had committed that this had befallen us. I am sure that beside me, many believers through the centuries have shared the experience of Job.

God allowed Job to experience pain to prove to the devil that in spite of what he suffered, Job would still be faithful. Job is the prime example of one who endured pain and suffering not because of wrong doing, but because of God. He used Job to model for Him. Whose model are you? Who are you making look good? There is a garment of suffering that God place upon many just to show forth His glory and power. A man was born blind in the book of Matthew, not because of the sins of his parents nor because he had done wrong. Jesus stated that he suffered blindness that he may show forth the power of God to heal blindness.

When life has pressed you to your lowest point and you think you can't go any lower, someone always comes along and push you even lower with discouraging words. I was so low; I could sit on a dime and swing my legs. Better yet, I was so low I could look up at the bottom.

What do you do when you hit rock bottom, when you can look up and the bottom is your top? When you hit rock bottom you have to stand on the Rock. That Rock is Jesus. By faith you have to see yourself on top. If you see it you can have it. Look to the hills from which cometh your help; your help cometh from the Lord. Faith will let you see the top even when you are on the bottom. Faith will let you see the end when you are still at the beginning.

A window of hope was opened for Job when a young man whom had sat and listened to his elders wrestle with Job as he sat on his heap of ash. Elihu, the youth, broke the linkage between sin and pain by pointing out that God at times use pain to instruct man.

Elihu did not explain why Job suffered, he just pointed out that in suffering, God may have a purpose that is separated from punishment, and many times He does. That statement single-handedly caused Job to return his heart to God and believe that God was good and would not act against His character.

Faith is your eyesight to the invisible.

What has pain taught you? It is a teacher. Pain can teach you compassion. I sat one day in church listening to the cry of a mother for her son. Her son had committed a crime and was serving time in prison. Tears fell from her face as she cried out for prayer concerning her son. Anger filled my heart as I said within myself, "How dare she ask for such a thing, her son did the crime let him do the time". God said, "You shall reap what you sow." It's easy to judge someone else when you haven't experienced their pain.

Years later I sat before a judge, fighting back tears, begging and pleading in silence for God to have mercy and pardon my son of his crime. I had stood before the church asking for prayer that God would grant him mercy. Pain filled my being as I sat in that courtroom watching my son being led away in a bright orange jumpsuit with his hands cuffed to his back. Now I felt the pain of that broken hearted mother who prayed the same prayer years earlier. Pain taught me to have compassion on others. You never know when sorrow and hurt will come to your house, and believe me it will come.

As you walk a mile in another person shoes, pain will teach you why they act the way they act. It will teach you why they said what they said. Understanding comes through pain. Now you know what you didn't know. Ministries are birthed out of pain. Brokenhearted mothers bring healing to other broken hearted mothers and abused wives bring healing to other abused wives.

God is the only one that I know who can bottle up all of your hurt, pains, disappointments, brokenness and tears and make something great out of it. God will instruct you in the mist of your pain to push. Push until your ministry comes forth. Push until life comes forth. Push until you come forth. Set your eyes on the glory that shall be revealed. Look beyond the cross. Hear the shout of those to whom your life of pain will bring healing. Look beyond the veil and you will see the glory of the Lord being made perfect through your pain.

If you see it you can have it.

Today you are in the birthing position and pain is invading your body. The pains are intense. It's as if you can't bear it any more. I serve notice to your spirit today; a ministry is about to come forth. Your pains are the sign that life is about to come into being. Your ministry is made out of your life's pains. Push, again I say, push. Bring your ministry into existence.

I live today because of yesterday's pains. I am the man I am today because of yesterday's pains. My ministry today was birthed out of yesterday's pains. No, there was nothing that felt good about it, but something good came about because of it. The devil meant it for bad, but God meant it for my good! Not only did something good come out of my pains, but I have also forgiven those who were the source of my pains.

Breakdown or Breakthrough

You have to make up in your mind that you will not allow the pains that others caused in your life to create reasons for you to breakdown. Tell the devil, "Before I breakdown I'll breakthrough"!

The plans of the enemy are to break you down. His weapon and strategy has changed; however, his objective is the same. The devil came to steal, kill, and destroy and he will use anything to break you down.

I am reminded of a military story. The Military trained personnel for "Special Services" to go behind the enemy line to gain special information during war time. One particular man was known as the million dollar man. Thousands of dollars was spent on him in combat training, weapons, and hand to hand training. Time after time he was successful in his assignment. His training carried him through the deadly time of war, escaping the hands of the enemy as he went into the battlefield. Later he retired a war hero and was decorated with the highest war metals of honor. Afterwards he bought a small house in a peaceful village at the foot of a snow caped mountain. The war was over and life was good.

One day while sitting in the village square, surrounded by the sounds of music and laugher, a young man dressed in find clothes walked by and shot him in the head with a small hand gun. The Military hero died in the village of his home after escaping the hands of him enemy a thousand times during war. How could this be? The million dollar man was dead. The enemy was successful because his approach, uniform, and weapon was different. The enemy uses the weapon of pain in order to get you to give up on life and turn your back on God and hold unforgiveness in your heart toward those who caused the pains.

While in the military, I was instructed during training that if I was ever captured by the enemy during war time there were several rules I had to follow. I was allowed only to give the enemy my name, rank and serial number. I was never to abandon my country and give the enemy information that would endanger my fellow soldier's lives. When captured, the enemy would interrogate you in order to get information from you.

Pressure will burst a pipe.

Interrogation is the method of interviewing a source used by personal to obtain information that the source would not otherwise willingly disclose. There are multiple possible methods of interrogation, which includes deception, increasing suggestibility, and using mind-altering drugs. However, the main source of interrogation is to apply pain. Pain would cause the person interviewed to "breakdown" and give the information needed or to cause the person to renounce their position. The devil will use pain in order to get you to breakdown and renounce your position in the body of Christ.

Special Notice

Every word that comes out of your mouth during interrogation will be tested. For this reason along, you must make sure that you can back up every word that you speak. The words of the king to the Three Hebrew Boys were, "Turn or burn. Give up your God and live, or hold on to Him and die the death of a fiery furnace." The king was interrogating God's children. He was trying to pressure them by threatening their lives with the pain of fear. The devil wants to put you under pressure and cause you to deny your God. He wants you to breakdown and collapse under pressure, falling apart by losing control of your mind. For this reason alone, let this mind be in you that was also in Christ Jesus.

The devil is trying to break you down! Your mind is under an attack and your faith is being tested. Pain is his weapon! What comes out of your mouth will be tested. The devil will put pressure on your testimony. The moment you say, "I will not go back to sin" will be the moment Satan will plan an attack of pain on your words.

What are you made of? Will you breakdown under the pressure of pain or will you breakthrough? Be careful what you say, it will be tested. You will be tested by pressure to see if you hold up or breakdown. The devil is out to make you break and your test will reveal what you are made of. The question is, "Will you breakthrough or breakdown?"

'Breakthrough' means to penetrate through. When we see the word "penetrate" it means to "break in"; therefore, breakthrough means to break in, in order to come through. In layman terms it means to have enough force, power, strength, and will, to break in and come out! To fight until you come through; advancing through and beyond the enemy's line of defense.

'Through' means from end to end of; from the beginning to the end of. We now have, breakdown, break in and break through. All three words have something in common; "BREAK". Whatever I do I will have to break. Break means to cause to come to pieces by a blow or push. Either way I choose to go I will be broken. So I might as well break in so I can breakthrough. I may just as well laugh as to cry because neither one of them will make a difference.

CHAPTER X

Life's Adversity

(Genesis 3:16) "Unto the woman he said, I will greatly multiply thy sorrow and thy conception; in sorrow thou shalt bring forth children; and thy desire shall be to thy husband, and he shall rule over thee."

In order to understand the relationship between life and pain we must go back to the first reference of pain in the Bible. The Word that was spoken to Eve was a principle that was established by God when He said that in pain thou shalt bare children. In layman terms God is saying, there is no bringing forth of life without pain. Pain is the doorway to life. Women throughout the world have experienced this painful process of giving birth. There is no birth without it.

The bringing forth of life is a painful course of action. Because of the pain involved in birth, many parents have decided to have only one child. In many cases mothers have even died in the process of giving birth. The Word that was spoken by God was a prophetic Word. Not only is this a natural principle, it is also a spiritual principle.

There is no birth without pain

Jesus stated in John 12:24 (KJV) "Very, very I say unto you, except a corn of wheat fall into the ground and die, it abideth alone: but if it die, it bringeth forth much fruit." Life is in the corn of wheat; however, it cannot come forth except the grain die. As being a born again believer, we have Life on the inside of us. There's no question about us obtaining life, the question is how to let this life come forth? This inward life can never come forth except the outward shell dies. It is important that the outer shell be broken. If the outward shell is never broken the inward life will never come forth. The question therefore is, "What is the outer shell and how can it be broken so life can come forth?" To better understand this question let's look at the seed.

A seed is a life giving potency.

What, exactly, is a seed? I don't mean what a seed looks like, or where do they come from, or what does a seed do. I mean what 'is' a seed? If you really understand seeds and exactly what a seed is, your chances of getting good results out of your life is greatly increased.

A seed is a life-giving potency launched by the parent plant, which carries the parent plant inside of it. In layman terms a seed is a part of the parent plant being launched out, or sent off from the parent plant that has the plant in it. It is launched in hope that it will eventually find itself in an agreeable place, right soil, right situation, and right place, in which it may develop, materialize and grow to maturity in order to produce fruits and yield more seeds of itself.

The very force of the seed's life lies inside the seed. That life driving force within the seed is stronger than any other force on earth. The life inside a seed will do whatever it has to do in order to come forth. It will come forth and reproduce itself. It's like a miracle, to plant a seed, and then have a harvest from the same seed that brings forth more seed of itself.

You are a seed and there's life inside of you. Inside of you is everything that you need to live. It's bottled up right now, but that life force will do whatever it has to do in order to come forth and reproduce itself. It's waiting for the right condition to form so that it can come forth.

Your conditions are the situations you are in or the ones you will face. Condition has everything to do with growth. In the natural four things must be present in order to make the condition right for a seed to grow. They are: water, oxygen, light and the right temperature. All four things must be acquired before growth occurs.

You are a seed and there's life inside of you.

There are several other things that a seed must also have in order to grow. The seed has to be planted. Plant is to be deposited in the ground. In the spiritual realm it means to deposit into someone or something. The situation you are in is a 'thing'. Your particular state of affairs is a thing. You are planted there so that you can grow. You are planted in that marriage so you can grow. You are planted in that ministry so that you can grow. A Seed cannot grow unless it is planted! You cannot grow unless you are planted! You are going through right now, but don't worry, you will come forth. If you keep going through you shall come out!

Your situations and state of affairs are the right soil for you to be planted. A seed has to be planted in soil. Each seed has a particular type of soil it has to be planted in. It is the soil that covers the seed and causes it to die. In order for it to die and bring forth itself in a new life it has to die.

Your situation that you are covered with is the soil that's going to kill the old you, but you will come forth a new creation. Once a seed is planted the soil has to be worked. Your situation will work you baby, work you. When you think you can't bare it any longer, more pain will come; the situation will become more difficult, the road will become rougher, and the hills will become taller. Don't worry you will come through!

Water- GOD'S SPIRIT- Just like a seed need certain things to help it come forth, you also need certain things to help you come forth. In the natural a seed need water. In the spirit you need water. Water is a symbol of God's Spirit. A seed will not be 'released' without water. You can never be released without God's Spirit. A seed cannot be released with a "little amount of water". If it were, it could risk coming to life in an area much too dry for survival. It needs to 'know' that the water supply is adequate to support it, until it can send its roots down to deep layers where there is most likely more moisture. You need to know that you have enough of God's Spirit inside of you in order to keep you in a desert land.

A Seed cannot be released with a little amount of water.

Germination begins when water penetrates the seed coat and initiates chemical changes within the tissues inside. Once the seed begin these changes, it can't be reversed. If the water supply stops and the process is unable to continue, the seed dies. You have to make up your mind and realize that you are on the road of no return and you can't give up now. If you stop the process you will die! You have enough of God's Spirit to bring you forth. Push!

A seed almost doubles in size in the process of taking up enough water for it to start germinating. The seed coat stretch slightly and then split, allowing more water and oxygen to come into contact with the contents and assist the growth. So you look a little different right about now; good, the Holy Spirit will make you look like that. You're acting strange. Well bless the Lord; you are being filled with God's sustaining power and you are about to give birth. Go on and stretch. Let the pressure come. Pressure will burst a pipe. When you break, more of God will come in and assist the growth of a new you.

Pressure will cause you to grow up.

Oxygen- (ANOINTING). Oxygen is very important to the chemical changes that go on inside as the seed germinates. These involve the changing of food storage substances into sugars and proteins, and then into amino acids. These amino acids are used to build up tissues of the up-and-coming plant. The process is called respiration, and it cannot take place without oxygen.

Balance is so important in development and growth. Wherever there's an intake there must also be an equal amount of outflow in order to balance the flow. This is called respiration. Respiration is the act of breathing air in and out. Air comes into the body in one form and exit the body in another form.

In your process of growing through, (I like to use the term 'growing through' because you are not just going through, you are growing in the process), you will receive the water (God's Spirit), that will fill you to the point of an overflow. That 'overflow' will be the Spirit of God exiting in another form. That form is called the anointing. It's the anointing that changes you from one form into another. From the inside out.

Light: (WORD). Light is another thing that helps release a seed. A seed needs to know that it is near the surface of the soil and not too far down for its shoot to reach the sun and air. The only thing a seed can tell is light and dark; a few inches might as well be a few feet. Darkness can have two effects on a seed; the seed will either die, or it can go to sleep and could live for thousands of years.

The Word will always pull toward Son-shine.

In your process of growing through the only thing you will recognize is light and darkness. Being covered with soil, you are well acquainted with darkness. What you need to come forth is light. Light is the Word.

(Psalm 119:105-112 KJV) "Thy word is a lamp unto my feet, and a light unto my path. I have sworn, and I will perform it, that I will keep thy righteous judgments. I am afflicted very much: quicken me, O Lord, according unto thy word. Accept, I beseech thee, the freewill offerings of my mouth, O Lord, and teach me thy judgments. My soul is continually in my hand: yet do I not forget thy law. The wicked have laid a snare for me: yet I erred not from thy precepts. Thy testimonies have I taken as a heritage forever: for they are the rejoicing of my heart. I have inclined mine heart to perform thy statutes always, even unto the end."

The Word will pull you through the darkness by pulling you toward it like the sun light pulls the shoot from a seed toward it. If you are too deep in the soil and your situation has killed you, don't worry, go to sleep. When the right season comes, you will come forth. It's just one of your processes of growth.

Temperature: (Right Season). Look like I can feel the breaking of day, O what joy springs forth in my soul. Every chemical process has a temperature range within which it can take place. If the temperature falls outside of that range, the reaction doesn't happen; when the right temperature comes the seed will come forth.

When it gets hot enough you will come forth. It hasn't got hot enough yet! Stay in the fire. There's reason for the fire. The fire comes to release you of everything that has you bound. As it was in the case with the Three Hebrew Boys so shall it be with thee. The only thing the fire did for the Hebrew boys was release them of their bondage. God is about to release you. It's not in the realm of your spirit or body that God is breaking, it in your soul.

The Bible place man as a trinity being, man is a spirit that has a soul that lives in a body (1 Thess. 5:23). When the Bible says we were created in God's image, it does not mean God looks like us; for God in essence is Spirit (John 2:24). We are like God in creative personality, having intellect, sensibility, and will. This likeness also refers to the Trinity of God. God is One in essence but three in "Person". The Father, Son and Holy Spirit. Man is one in essence but three in being, spirit, soul and body.

God is a soul breaker.

The body is the earth suit that houses the spirit and soul of man. Man's spirit and soul lives in the body. As becoming a born again believer only your spirit is born of God. Your body and soul remain the same. The battle that we have as being believers is not in our spirit. The battle is in the soul. The soul is the shell. In the soul is the place where our will, feelings, emotions and thoughts live. It is for this reason that as being born again believers we must renew our minds; for the mind house the ways and thought pattern of the old man (Romans 12:2).

Your born of the Father's Spirit is at war with your will, feeling, emotion and thoughts. The pain that we are dealing with is in the soul. Before becoming believers we were led by our soul; by the way we felt and thought. We were led by our bodies, doing what felt good. Now as being a born again believer, your spirit is struggling to come forth and take its proper place as being led by the Spirit of God, its Creator. Except the soul dies the spirit will never come forth.

What is this death? This death is the dying to ones will, ways, feelings, emotions and thoughts. This death comes about after you have been born again by the Spirit of God. Life will never come forth until this death takes place. When we speak of "life" we are in reference to the new you. You will never come forth until your soul is broken and God will use any and everything to bring your soul to that place of brokenness.

There is nothing that can hinder us from coming forth, as to that of the soul. Your "feelings" are one of your biggest enemies that will keep you from coming forth. The pain of misunderstanding, envy, hatred, wrath and strife must be put to death. Your, "Hurt my feelings", must die.

The devil control many believers today through the channel of their feelings. You will never become the person you were born to be until you surpass the soul. It is sad to say but most believers operate out of their soul and not out of their spirit. Their spirits are struggling to come forth; however, the pain of death to one's old ways, will and desires hinder the birth.

A young boy watched a man carve a log into the figure of a person. The young boy in amazement said, "I didn't know he was in the log." The carver said to the boy, "He was there all the time; however, he had to be brought forth." The log had to first stop being the log in order for it to become the figure of a person.

You were born again to become someone.

The pain is in the cutting away of those things that will hinder us from being born or better yet, from coming forth. It is one thing to be born again; however, it's another thing to come forth. In other words, to become what you were born again to become. You were born again to become someone. Are you that someone you were born again to become?

Why were you born again? Were you born again to get something or to become something? We are born again to become what God created man to be from the beginning. We are not born again just to be "saved".

Once you are saved there is someone God wants you to be. The process of becoming that person comes after salvation.

The pain of life comes after salvation. Though you may be saved, there is some cutting away God has to do. The pains of life are the tools that will cause you to come forth. Even as God spoke in the beginning, so shall it be in the end. In much pain, thou shall bring forth children. The new you will come forth through much pain. Push, for the new you are about to come forth, again I say PUSH!

CHAPTER XI

It Doesn't Hurt Anymore

2 Corinthians 12:8-10 (KJV) "Concerning this thing I pleaded with the Lord three times that it might depart from me. And He said to me, "My grace is sufficient for you, for My strength is made perfect in weakness." Therefore most gladly I will rather boast in my infirmities, that the power of Christ may rest upon me. Therefore I take pleasure in infirmities, in reproaches, in needs, in persecutions, in distresses, for Christ's sake. For when I am weak, then I am strong."

What is this I feel? So much adversity! Life is so hard! My soul cries out for relief but there seems to be none. Pain! Pain! Pain! What is happening to me? Am I a sacrifice? Why so much trouble? I try to explain but no one seems to hear. I feel like I have been picked out to be picked on. Where can I hide? I want to run away but there's no place to run. No place to hide.

Why is it that after many years of adversities many people still don't change? Day after day the weather reporter let us know the state of the weather. Tomorrow there will be showers. Day after day we get wet. Why? The reason is because we choose not to do anything to keep from getting wet. Put on your raincoat!

Repeatedly people are in situations; no matter what they do or say the situations remain the same. You pray and God for reasons unknown to you, chooses not to answer your prayer. When God doesn't answer prayers, there's something God is doing for "you", in the situation.

In II Cor. 12:8, Paul prayed three times and asked God to remove his thorn in the flesh and God declined to do so. There was something God was doing for Paul in the situation. There is something God is doing to you in your situation. When you pray and God doesn't give a yes or no, He's still answering. When there's neither a yes or no, God is saying wait, stay where you are. Do nothing! Even in silence God speaks.

As a pastor, I have seen many people in bad relationships. I have heard their cries. I have felt their pains. I have witnessed their brokenness. The thing that amazes me the most is how God takes bad relationships and use them to change people. God use pain to transform a person into the individual He desires them to be. There's a person inside of you that God wants to come forth; however, that individual will never come forth without the process of pain. Pain is a sign of new life coming forth. There's a new you about to be born.

Hell will cause you to change.

In most instances God is not trying to change situations because God can speak and the situation will change. God wants to change you in the situation. In many cases the situation will never change. What do you do when the situation doesn't change? You change! If you know that it's going to be storms in your life, put on your rain coat, hat and boots and go through it.

Though the storm is still there it doesn't affect you. God is using your troublesome marriages, relationships, jobs and family members to change YOU! Pains are filling your life. The Lord is saying, "Good!" It's good for you that trouble come. It's good that pain comes. Trouble and pain will cause you to do something. Believe it or not, God will lead you into turmoil and pains.

The thing with most believers is, they do not know when God is leading them. Just because something isn't good doesn't mean God's name is attached to it. God will lead you into the very portholes of hell. It's not for hell's sake you are there; it's for your sake that you are there.

Hell is not going to change but hell will cause you to change. There are characteristics that God is developing in you and hell is bringing it about. Your bad marriage is causing you to change into the person God wants you to be.

Believe me when I say, there are situations that God will not release you from. He will employ it to mature you. There is a person God has connected me with that has caused me much pain; yet, God would not release me, no matter how I prayed. God was using that situation to change Apostle Milton Adams. When there are characteristics in you that need to be removed, God will allow situations to come that will push those characteristics to the surface. You don't know what you have or what you can do until test time comes.

God gave Joseph dreams as a young boy of his family bowing down to him (Genesis 37). As a young boy, Joseph wasn't ready for this position. There were characteristics in Joseph that had to be removed. The pit and prison made Joseph ready for the palace. Your pit and prison are making you ready for your palace.

Today you are the problem; tomorrow you shall be the solution. Today you serve the man and woman of God, tomorrow you shall be the man or woman of God. Today you stand at the door and greet people; tomorrow you shall stand behind the pulpit and preach to nations. Today you give your last; tomorrow someone will give you their last. Today it hurt; tomorrow there shall be no pain!

No more milk, its meat time!

The thing about being the problem is we don't see ourselves as the problem. We see everything else but ourselves. It's common not to see self because self is in the place where you are. You have to look inside to see self. Your job, wife, husband, in-laws and church are not the problem. You are the problem and God is bringing you to a place of matureness!

Recess is over and it's time to come in off of the playground. Your days on the merry-go-round are over. Spinning your wheels and going nowhere! The days of swinging are over; up today down tomorrow. It's time to grow up. No more milk, its meat times!

David was anointed king as a young shepherd boy by the prophet Samuel while attending sheep in his father's house; however, David did not enter into kingdom-ship until he was a mature man (1 Samuel 16:13).

God is moving you toward that place of matureness. The reason God has not given you what you ask is because you can't manage it yet. God wants to get you to the place where you can manage what He has for you; to the place where those things that were important to you doesn't matter anymore. Where the pain doesn't hurt anymore!

When you get to the place where you enjoy serving others you are ready for others to serve you. When you get to the place where you love people, you are now ready to lead the lowest. What's inside of me that God's bringing out?

What lack I yet? A young rich ruler came to Jesus in Matthew 19th chapter and asked, "What shall I do to inherit eternal life?" Jesus responded by saying, "Keep the commandments." The young ruler stated, "I have done these things from a youth until now, "What lack I yet"? Jesus told the rich ruler to sell all that he had and give it to the poor. The rich ruler walked away for the price was too great. For the rich ruler to sell all he had and give it away was to become poor; to become like those around him, a place of dying, lifting others higher than himself.

What a question to ask Jesus, "What lacking I yet?" Never ask Him if you are not ready for His answer. He will always bring you to a place of death; the place where you die. When something is dead it ceases from being; it's not active nor is it productive, yielding nothing, having no power, spirit or feeling. In simple term it's lifeless. John put it this way, "I must decrease so He can increase" (John 3:30 KJV). I must come to a place of death so that He can come alive in me.

Anyone who follows Jesus will come to the place where they will discover that their greatest hindrance is not others but self. God use others to reveal to us our weakness and strength by shining light on those things that will hinder us from operating in the realm of the Spirit. The problem is not with your spirit it's with your soul.

In the soul realm is where you deal with feelings, emotions and your will. Your soul has to be broken. You will never come forth until you are broken in your soul. Your feelings have to die. You have to surpass your emotions. Your feelings and emotions are enemies to your spirit. They will lead you away from God. They will keep you from being born the person God wants you to be. The pain and hurt that you are feeling is not your spirit crying out, it's your soul saying, "I am hurting!" It's your soul crying out from the pain of death. Your soul doesn't want to die. Crucify your feelings and live!

God is bringing you to a place where it doesn't matter anymore. The soul has been broken, the pains are there but the hurt is gone. No longer are your feelings and emotions leading you. Your spirit is in control! What use to hurt doesn't hurt any more. Last year I would have cracked. This year I am shouting. Last year I would have crawled into bed in a fetus position and went into depression. Today I walk through the valley of the shadow of death. I fear no evil for God is with me. Last year I would have cried, today I laugh. No, the situation hasn't changed. The same thing is going on in your life, in your home, on your job, in your family. Things may not change; howbeit, they will change you! No more up today and down tomorrow. No more spinning my wheels and going nowhere. God will bring you into your season of matureness. It's no more milk, its meat time! It doesn't hurt any more.

It was never others; they have never been "my" problem. My problem has always been me. God only used others to bring you to the place where He desired for you to operate. Is it painful? Yes! However, you will become stronger today because others brought hell out of you. God knows who to put in your life. Glory! The other person is only there to bring hell out of you. That hell will force you, make you, and cause you to move into the position where God wants you to operate. Good things can come out of bad situations.

There's a reason for everyone being in your life. The question is why are they there? There's a reason why you are on your particular job. The question is why are you there? The Bible said that the steps of a righteous man are order by God (Psa. 37:23 KJV). God has ordered your life for you. He knows what to put in your life to bring you to the point of death.

I was told that child bearing is very painful. In giving birth, the pain becomes so intense that you think you can't take it anymore. The moment you think you can't bear it any more is the moment the child comes. So you think you can't bear it any more. PUSH! There's a new you about to come forth. Push until you come forth.

CHAPTER XII

Silent Night Cries

Psalm 3:1-8 (KJV) "LORD, how they are increased that trouble me! Many are they that rise up against me. Many there be which say of my soul, there is no help for him in God. Selah. But thou, O LORD, art a shield for me; my glory, and the lifter up of mine head. I cried unto the LORD with my voice, and he heard me out of his holy hill. Selah. I laid me down and slept; I awaked; for the LORD sustained me. I will not be afraid of ten thousands of people that have set themselves against me round about. Arise, O LORD; save me, O my God: for thou hast smitten all mine enemies upon the cheek bone; thou hast broken the teeth of the ungodly. Salvation belongeth unto the LORD: thy blessing is upon thy people. Selah.

The darkness of the house carries the pain of many silent nights; pains that will never surface or be heard by any one. Pains that will cause a boy or girl to grow up and become a dysfunctional person, dealing with feelings and emotions that cannot be explained; crying a silent cry that no one hears, afraid to show their scars because their wounds are still open and tender from a lack of proper healing. The sadness in their eyes reflects the brokenness of an abused and used soul. Their silent cry is,"

I am broken, will you please heal me?" However, the question remains, "Who can heal me?"

These cries rang from the walls of houses throughout this land, hurting souls that have no safe haven. Their refuge is found in their minds by blocking out the terror of the night. Later they discover they are labeled slow and unable to grasp things because of this blockage that came about through the pains of a silent night. Who can heal me?

Rick Nauert Ph.D. Senior News Editor Reviewed by John M. Grohol, Psy.D. on June 3, 2013 stated in his writing Brain Changes from Child Abuse Tied to Adult Mental Illness, Sexual Problems, that different types of childhood abuse can increase the risk of mental illness as well as sexual dysfunction, experts say, but the life change by which this occurs has been unknown. New research may provide an answer with the discovery that sexually abused and emotionally mistreated children exhibit specific and differential changes in the architecture of their brain. In the study, an international team of researchers discovered that brain changes reflect the nature of the mistreatment. Researchers have known that victims of childhood abuse often suffer from psychiatric disorders later in life, including sexual dysfunction following sexual abuse. The underlying mechanisms facilitating this association have been poorly understood. Charles B. Nemeroff, M.D., Ph.D. and a group of scientists hypothesized that brain or cortical changes during segments of mistreatment played a role.

I washed my fish tank one night and filled it to the brim with fresh water. I sat and watched the fish swim back and forth as they enjoyed the fresh moment. Sleep called and I answered. Upon waking the following morning, I discovered that several of the fish had leaped from the tank and had died during the night. No one heard their cries, however they cried. No one felt their pains, nevertheless they suffered. No one saw their strugglers, yet they made great effort to live. While the silence of the night brought pleasure to me, it brought the pains of death to my fish. During the silent night, pain came and no one heard it. What were they thinking?

While others sleep, souls are crying out. The pains of a silent night have brought much hurt, and to many it has brought death. As it was with my fish, no one heard their cries nor saw their strugglers. A cry was made and there was a fight to live, but no one noticed. Who can heal me?

A twelve year old boy lay silent in bed resting from a hard day of picking cotton in the hills of Mississippi. His back ached from pulling a nine-foot sack about his shoulders during the day, packing it with cotton from end to end. Life on the farm was hard labor for everyone. The day brought about hard work in the fields, cutting firewood, feeding the hogs, milking the cows and carrying water from the spring in old tin molasses buckets. These were his daily odd jobs. Everyone welcomed the falling nights. "Thank God, it's night and now I can rest", were his thoughts as he crawled into the bed that had been assigned to him.

Being the son of a sharecropper, it was no strange thing for his father to let him and his brothers stay with other members of the church to help them with their field work. It was a delight to spend time at other people houses. The only other places a country boy could go were church and school. However, a delightful moment could turn into a life time of horror.

Everyone fought for the best position as three to four would bunk together in one bed. The hard task of the day caused everyone to fall fast asleep; at least that's what was thought. The night held terror that was beyond any child's barren mind.

He could feel the breath of another one breathing heavily upon his neck. His breath smelt from the stink that filled his unhealthy mouth. The sound of his breathing pierced the very soul of a child; fear griped his very being as his face was being touched by another.

Afraid to open his eyes, he lay as still as he possibly could as tears filled the heart of his soul. "No, not again", He cried silently within as he flashed back to earlier days of abuse. His hand was rough, hard and coarse. He could feel knots inside of it that had developed from the hard labor of farm work as he stroked his body.

Beware of false prophets, which come to you in sheep's clothing, but inwardly they are ravening wolves.

Slowly he moved the cover from his body as he tried desperately not to awaken him nor disturb others that were fast asleep. A wolf in sheep clothing was he. It was only a few hours earlier this pervert's hands were raised as if to praising the Lord. Beware of false prophets that come to you in sheep clothing for inwardly they are raving wolves seeking a weak prey.

Slowly his hand stroked the inside of the child's thigh as he worked his hand into the leg of his shorts. The child's heart pounded as his body shook from fear. With every ounce of strength he had, he tried desperately not to let him know that he was aware of what was going on, not knowing what he would do. Why? Why didn't he cry out? Because of fear! Fear is a very powerful force. It will make you do what you never dreamed you would do. Of all the forces in this world there's none like that of pain and fear, except love. Who can heal this child?

What is this force that controlled him? Fear! Fear is a basic emotional sensation and response feeling by a strong dislike to some perceived risk or threat. Fear also can be described as a feeling of extreme dislike towards certain conditions, objects, people, or situations such as: fear of darkness, fear of ghosts, or fear of a particular type of touch. Personal fear varies extremely in degree from mild caution to extreme dislike of something. This was a strong dislike for this country child.

As this pervert fondled his private parts the boy could feel his body shaking with uncontrollable movements. Ignorant on what he was doing, the boy discovered later that the pervert was masturbating. Unknown to the boy's father, he had left his son in the hands of a church going, sex pervert that molested young boys. Afterward the pervert would take his hand and put his wet substance all over the private parts of the child, as he breathed heavily from his sexual pleasure. A wolf in sheep clothing.

Wolves in the Church

Wolves in the church are not a new thing and it will never become an old thing either. It will always be. They live in and around the church. We are living in days of great deception; more than ever it seems. Churches today are filled with many so called pretending Christians and religious people who are living spiritually defeated lives such as adultery, lust, premarital sex, addicted to pornography and sexual fantasies, tobacco, alcohol etc. Sexual predators and offenders who are committing sexual sins are increasing in a strong way inside and outside churches who are violating God's Laws and God's children.

Satan is actively working inside many churches today to destroy the people of God. Satan himself masquerades as an angel of light .No wonder his followers deceive others in the name of God, Church and Jesus Christ. Many have disguised themselves as the children of Christ and appear to be very passionate workers of God, but actually they are being the servants of Satan have the appearance of sanctity but inwardly they are evil,greedy, corrupted, dangerous, sex starved hypocrites, boastful, manipulative, bearing evil fruits which are of the devil. They are the wolves who pretend to be sheep and their real intent is to devour the flock.

Two Types of Wolves

There are two kinds of wolves, wolves outside the church and wolves inside the church. Paul stated, "For I know this that after my departing shall grievous wolves **enter in among you**, not sparing the flock (Acts 20:29 KJV). Paul spoke about wolves as being a certainty. They will "enter in among you", meaning they are not already in the church. These types of wolves usually wait until the leader is absent to enter. They realize the leader is likely to have discernment of spirits and can spot them.

Paul also stated, "Even from your own number men will arise and distort the truth in order to draw away disciples after them (Acts 20:30 KJV). These are the most dangerous kind, because they are already in the church, and therefore the most difficult to deal with. These types of wolves always operate behind the backs of the leaders. They will often visit church members in their homes without the knowledge of the church leaders. Lots of these wolves also have obtained authority or position in the church and use their power to deceive those who are not strong in the Lord.

How can a twelve year old boy tell his daddy that a member of the church is sexually molesting him at night? Will it cause problems to develop between two families? Will his daddy believe him? These questions raced rapidly through his mind as he sought daily for answers.

Why didn't he stop him from molesting him? Where did this fear come from? The answer was about to be exposed.

Earlier in this child's childhood he had felt the handprints of another male upon his body. Many today struggle with the hurt of a broken and bent soul. He feels the hurt and abuse of others and reaches out to bring healing. Why, because I was that child and I understand. People can pierce your very being, walk away and never say I'm sorry. Healing has to take place. Who can heal the child?

Because of who the person was that molested me earlier, I tried to block the experience out of my mind. I can still smell the scent from his private part as he forced it about my face. There was no remorse as he enjoyed the moment. More than anything in this world I wished he would die. Anger filled my very being. I would never forgive him. Who can heal me?

Those who do not forgive will not be forgiven.

I often wonder, "Why did God put such a task upon His children? To love their enemy, pray for those who use you, forgive those who wrong you". So unfair it appears to be and in all truth it is. What's fair about, "If I don't forgive than I am not forgiven". We'll understand it better bye and bye.

Children today live the experience of a silent night's cry. Their minds are twisted from a lack of identity. "Who am I", is their cry. Why is it that I feel the way I do about particular sexual desires. Confused minds and perplex thoughts seeks to control their every move. Who can heal me?

I hated myself as I grew in my childhood. I was labeled slow because I was unable to grab hold to things quickly. My brain was twisted. My understanding was very unfruitful. Little did people know that the hands of others had twisted my child like mind. My first sexual experience was that of a man. It was supposed to be that of a woman, the way God created it to be. Bitterness and unforgiveness filled my very being. I was broken and was in need of much healing. The silence of the nights brought me much pain that no one ever heard.

Why Should I Forgive?

The sad thing about housing unforgiveness is the fact that you will become controlled by it or by the person that caused you harm. It will put you in bondage. Unforgiveness will cause spirits to become attracted to what caused the unforgiveness inside of you. Because of the unforgiveness in my heart other child molesters and sex perverts became attracted to my wounded spirit. Like flies are attracted to the fragrance of filth, so are spirits attracted to the odor of a wounded soul. For this reason every wound needs to be healed. Who can heal me? Who can heal the bitterness of a wounded soul?

Forgiveness is necessary to avoid entrapment by Satan. I have discovered in ministry and in my counseling that unforgiveness is the number one avenue Satan uses to gain entrance to believers' lives. Paul encouraged mutual forgiveness 'in order that no advantage be taken of us by Satan; for we are not ignorant of his schemes' (2 Cor. 2:11 KJV). Unforgiveness is an open invitation to Satan's bondage in our lives. For this reason alone you must let go, get over it, move on and begin again. God knows that forgiveness frees His children.

I am the first to say, "I'm so sorry for all that has hurt each of you". I mean no disrespect or harm by my comments, I simply want to share how God is setting me free from that which has hurt me. And I know that many of you who serves in leadership roles that have been hurt and are responsible for much. The fact is that unforgiveness will weaken your ability to provide balance in your leadership.

You may be wondering why you are struggling with sins you thought came out of nowhere. You may be struggling with random outbursts of anger you can't explain. You may think you can control the beast of unforgiveness that slowly and strategically grows within you, but you will not win this battle on your own. You must cry out to Jesus and allow Him to heal your heart. You must allow him to remove the toxin that someone else's sin against you has deposited in your soul. You can be healed, you can be free, but God will not force Himself on you. You must want healing more than vengeance.

Forgiving is the door to your healing.

Deliverance from the Past

Years later I was the invited speaker of a revival service. The church was filled to the overflow as the Spirit of God moved mightily among the believers. My message that night was about the control of unforgiveness. At the closing of the message I invited those up who was in need of healing from the past and the releasing of unforgiveness. One by one they came forth; God brought deliverance.

All of a sudden I looked and there he stood right before me, the man that had molested me as a child. He had come for prayer. Eye to eye we stood facing one another. My heart raced a hundred miles an hour. I waited a moment. Maybe he'll ask for forgiveness. However, the words, "I'm sorry, please forgive me" never fell from his lips. I waited so long to hear them, but they never came. As of today, they have never come and they never will from him. He's dead.

How can I put my hand upon one that caused so much hurt? How can I touch him? What is this that I feel inside of me? Could it be unforgiveness? My soul cried out, "It's not fair!" How dare he stand before me with no shame and ask me for pray? Go to hell was the words I sought to say. My heart pounded heavily. Inside the preacher that was the invited guest of a Spirit filled revival was unforgiveness. I too was struggling to be free from the pains of a silent night as I prayed for others to be delivered.

Quickly I put my arms around him, pulling him close to my chest. Tears filled my eyes as I held him closely. Softly I whispered in his ear saying, "I forgive you." His head dropped in the lock of my shoulder as tears rolled down his cheeks. No, he never said, "I'm sorry, please forgive me", But the look in his eyes said it all.

Deliverance came into my life after I released him and others for hurting me. By doing so, I released myself from the bondage of a silent night. No one has ever asked for forgiveness and maybe never will. It doesn't matter! There are things in life you just have to get over without the help of anyone else. You have to let it go.

There are those who will never hear the words I'm sorry, forgive me for what I've done to you. Believe me when I say I feel your pains. I know where you are. My eyes also reflect the hurts of a silent night's pain, and yes I also long to hear those words fall from the lips of those who caused me harm. I also walk with a limp because I was once dropped. We all have our limps. Nevertheless, you cannot allow your pass to dictate your future. You cannot afford to be hurt in the past and live the rest of your life in the future of bondage to those pains. Set yourself free and bring healing to yourself by forgiving and releasing those who harm you in your night of silent pains.

No One Asked For Forgiveness

You might ask, "Why forgive when no one asks"? I often refer to the parable of the Prodigal Son when asked this question. For many of us the focus is upon the son who left home and went into a strange land, spending all of his possession, returning home into the arms of an awaiting father; however, there was another son who is mentioned only once in the story. Upon the return of his brother, anger filled his heart because of the warm greeting of his father toward his no-good, woman-chasing, irresponsible, money-spending brother. I know, it sounds like someone you know.

The elder brother has always done what he was supposed to do. He has played by the rules, obeyed his father, and worked himself to the bone. Does this remind you of yourself, always doing what was asked but yet getting the short end of the stick? I can see why he was upset when the reprobate son shows up one day seeking to get back into the father's house. What's the point of always doing what you're supposed to do if it doesn't earn you favor? It is easy for me to imagine the elder son feelings being hurt every time he sees his no-good brother walking around in the house in his new robe and showing off his gold ring.

To get a better picture you have to understand that forgiveness of a child comes much easier for a parent than for a sibling. What loving father wouldn't forgive a disobedient son who returns home broken and humble, no matter how rebellious he had been? There is nothing remarkable in that. The truth of forgiveness in the story comes into play when we look at the older son. He too must forgive his younger brother, and it will be much harder for him than for his dad. And, what's more, he may also have to forgive his father. Now I know that this doesn't make much sense if we only think of forgiveness as 'receiving' pardon for hurting or doing someone wrong. So what's to forgive?"

Forgiveness set the forgiver free.

To better answer this question let's look at what forgiveness is. Forgiveness means giving up and turning over. It's that simple. To give up or turn over something is to release whatever power it holds over you. In my forgiving those for wronging me, I no longer allowed what they did to determine how I treat other people. I may remember the wrong, and I certainly do, but I have disarmed it. It no longer controls my actions, thoughts, or words. So this is the reason why you forgive, or better yet, this is the reason why you release it, because truly only Jesus can forgive sin. You release it so that you can be free, and liberated from the negative power they had over you. Forgiveness sets you free! In releasing his brother for what he did the older son was free from his anger and bitterness. The problem was not only in the younger son, the problem was inside of the oldest son too. It took this to show the elder the problem that he had on the inside of him.

A disliked rule

There's a rule for forgiveness that I truly dislike. Jesus said, "Forgive us our debts, as we also have forgiven our debtors". Luke put it this way, "Forgive us our sins, for we ourselves forgive every one indebted to us." In layman terms it means, "Forgive me according to the way I forgive others." I've said many times to the Lord, "This is not fair." God put me in check when He asked me, "What is fair and who determines fairness?" Fair is free from favoritism or self-interest or bias or deception, conforming to established standards of rules. According to this definition, fair is based upon an established rule. God sets the rules. If you don't like the rule play another game.

Fairness is not based upon our feelings or upon our willingness to forgive. Fairness is based upon God's rules. We are forgiven according to the way we forgive. Do I like it? No! A thousand times, no! I don't forgive because 'I like it.' I forgive because that's the rule, plus I need much forgiveness.

Easier said than done

I know that to forgive is easier said than done, rule or no rule. Someone had violated and hurt me. I am the one who's in pain and in need of help. How can I heal others when I'm in need of healing?

Don't play the fool

A fool is one who is tricked or deceived by bad judgment. If there's one thing the enemy would like more than anything else is to trick you into living those same pains and hurts over and over again. Many believe that forgiveness is putting yourself back into the same position to get hurt again. This is by far wrong. Remember, forgiving is to give up or turn over something by releasing whatever power it holds over you.

Forgiving someone doesn't mean putting them back in a situation where they can do the same thing again. If a man has a problem with stealing and has stolen from you, forgiving him is releasing him of the pains he caused you in the pass, not giving him a key and putting him back in your house. That's unwise! Let them know, with God's help, that you forgive but don't trust. Don't wear a mask like everything is ok when it's not. Don't live your life behind a mask afraid to express.

Living behind the Mask

Because of certain incidents in one's life they quickly put on masks to cover the shame and guilt. Believe it or not, we all wear masks. The thing that a mask does is change the identity of the wearer; however, changing the identity is not the same as transforming it. The mask only covers up what's there, allowing the person to replace ones reality with another by concealing and changing, the "person" behind the image into something or someone else other than who they are. However, the change of identity that a mask produces is always exterior and temporary. Although the change can be a deep-seated one, there is no philosophical transformation of the person behind the mask. When the mask is removed, the person remained unchanged anyway.

The one wearing the mask has not been transformed by the mask. Think of any of the masked characters of your childhood; my best-liked was Batman! He would put on his mask in order to enter into another role, totally different than his natural self. The businessman Bruce Wayne changed behind his mask into the super-hero, Batman. But Bruce Wayne remains untransformed. When the mask is removed, he returns to his former self and life-style. Does this sound like someone you know, maybe yourself?

Masks are often worn to conceal a person's undesirable and unholy characteristic called unforgiveness. We all want to be accepted and loved. There are things in everyone's life that we wish we could change. Many ordinary people put on invisible masks in their unsuccessful attempts to shield themselves from others. But wearing a mask fails to transform you. With mask on or off, you still remain basically the same. Burglars and thugs hide behind masks in an attempt to conceal their physical appearance and identity. But once again, although the mask changes their appearance for a time, there is no transformation of their true self.

Transformation is a mind thing. Transformation means to be transformed from one fashion, or person, into a total different one. This transformation takes place in the soul realm. Romans 12: 2 KJV "Be not conformed to this world, but be ye transformed by the renewing of the mind." Change the way a man thinks, you can transform the man.

I have learned that when a mask is used by a person in order to deceive others, its use is then dishonest and dangerous. A person who is wearing a 'mask of deception', if I may call it that, has the capability of inflicting a great deal of harm, pain and damage onto others and themselves. One can easily fall in love with the mask and not the real person behind the mask. No matter how I felt. No matter even if I felt that I wanted to burst into tears and tell someone to go to hell for all the pain they caused me, I always felt that I had to present myself as having it all together and no unforgiveness housed this soul. After all, so many others depended upon Milton's strength. At least that's what I thought. So I would put on my mask, smile and say all the right things. No one ever knew that I felt very different than how I looked.

Where did this come from? I can remember when we were moving from the country to town when I was about twelve years old. There wasn't enough room for everyone in the borrowed car to go, so I put my mask on to be the family hero and stayed behind so there would be room for all the others. Outwardly I appeared to be brave and fearless; my mask covered the scared boy that lived inside. After all, I was the prophet that prophesied we would move to town. If anyone stayed, I would be the family sacrifice, that others would be happy. Today I still fight to remove this mask of being the family hero.

I felt important, I was the family hero. Everyone was made happy because of my sacrifice. No one made me wear my mask; however, it felt as if it was forced upon me because no one wanted to stay. And beside why should everyone be unhappy when one can make all happy, even if they were unhappy?

I can recall in the movie Spiderman when Peter Parker became Spiderman. Because of his fear that everyone around him was and would in some way continue to get hurt because of who he was, he chose not to be Mary James's boyfriend. He became unhappy in order to save the one he truly loved.

You can very easily find yourself trapped in being what God never created you to be, just to feel important, to protect someone, or to be well-liked. You never chose to live in a state of deception and you never chose to live in a state of emotional and mental suffering. Yet, that's where you found yourself!

You were a victim and were trapped. Choice didn't even come into play until you began to realize something was wrong and began to question your unhappiness. Then, you are faced with the choice to either remain living like that, so others can be happy, or to make a change. Believe me when I say, "That's a choice that is never an easy one to make." Why, you may ask? Because no one ever knew the real you and now you are afraid that if you remove your mask, people may not like what they see and you will not be accepted.

I often think about the super hero Superman hiding behind the eyeglasses of Clark Kent. Clark Kent was not well liked by Lois Lane. Lois fell in love with Superman not knowing she had really fallen in love with Clark Kent. Once she found out that Clark Kent was really Superman she loved Clark. Question, "Did she love Clark Kent for Clark Kent or because she found out he was Superman?" The other thing about Clark Kent was, he didn't have to hide behind the glasses of Clark Kent. He was Superman with or without the glasses. He could have won Lois' love as Clark Kent.

Sometimes people don't want you to pull your mask off. They don't want you to change. They love what they are getting. They are happy. Now you are a victim of deception and manipulation. The cost of quitting, spiritually and emotionally can be too frightening to entertain. Until you become totally convinced that you are the one being deceived and manipulated, you will never remove your mask. The masks have become your norm. Until you realize that you can safely 'put away the mask' and live, you can never 'get on with life'.

You cannot live up to everyone's expectation. You will not always be able to keep every promise you make. Yes, people will hold things over your head; however, there're no super-heroes. We are only people whose traveling life's road in search of destiny. In doing so, you will miss the ball sometimes. You will disappoint people sometimes. You are sure to make mistakes sometimes. Howbeit, life goes on. You must learn to live again! If you had known, maybe you would have done things differently. Howbeit, you didn't know.

Overcoming guilt and beginning once again to live can be the one thing that some never anticipated would happen after they have failed. The truth is however, that whether we like it or not life continues on. The decision that we need to make is whether we wish to move on with life. The devil wants you to live with carrying this guilt bag around all your life, feeling bad about not pleasing people. If you are to live again you cannot be a people pleaser. You must become a God pleaser. WOW, how did I get so far off into that? Guess someone needed that. Spirit written.

CHAPTER XIII

It's All Good

Proverbs 4:23 (KJV) "Keep your heart with all diligence for out of it are the issues of life"

Humpty Dumpty sat on a wall. Humpty Dumpty had a great fall. All the King's horses, and all the King's men, couldn't put Humpty Dumpty back together again. What do you do with scrambled eggs? You make an omelet, eat it and enjoy the meal.

Proverbs 18:14 (KJV) "The spirit of a man will sustain his infirmity; but a wounded spirit who can bear?

A wounded spirit needs healing. Many people use anger and revenge to respond to hurt. Anger, in its practical sense, is a wish to harm the person that hurt you. And you do want to hurt those who hurt you by getting revenge. This I can testify too. Revenge is an act of carrying out that hurt in some way. Revenge can be carried out through words, or it can be carried out through violence. But, like hiding the hurt, anger and revenge do not heal the hurt. That's because all hurt, at its core, is simply a reminder of your human weakness and helplessness. You need help dealing with the hurt. Even if you kill the person who hurts you,

you still remain vulnerable to another attack from someone else. With all of your anger and revenge, you might temporarily feel good, but the feeling is just a figment of your imagination. The real you is still hurting and need healing. No matter what you do, you remain vulnerable to be attacked from someone else, anytime and anywhere because of your wounded spirit. And if you aren't healed, you will be attacked again. Allow me to say it again, "You will be hurt again", because the devil can smell your open-wounded-spirit.

The devil can smell a wounded soul

As a hunter, I have noticed that in wounding an animal, without a kill, the animal whole objective is to bring hurt to the one who caused the hurt. And if the wound remains open other prey will also attack the animal because of that open wound. The devil is the same way; he can smell and will attack your open-wounded-spirit. And you can rest assured; he knows how to hit where it hurts the most.

Blessed be the Lord on high, in spite of all our human reactions and foolishness we have another option. Instead of attacking the one who caused the pains, we can use our pains.

When we are hurt, we don't have to fight back, trying to hurt others as they have hurt us. We can trust in God's perfect justice to protect us. I have watched each person that caused me harm as a child receive justice from God. And I must say, "Justice is not always an appealing picture". In spite of our injuries, we must give understanding, patience, compassion, mercy, and forgiveness to those who hurt us, all while praying that they will repent of their wickedness.

When I was first hurt, I prayed that each person would go to hell with gasoline shorts on. Today I pray for mercy and house no unforgiveness in my heart toward others. I have used my pain to bring healing to others.

For My Good

Today as I reflect back over my life, I ask the question, "What was Satan's plan"? Of a certainty, he meant it for my bad; God meant it for my good. I often think about Joseph and the word he stated to his brothers. "I am Joseph your brother, whom ye sold into Egypt. Now therefore be not grieved, nor angry with yourselves. That ye sent me hither: for God did send me before you to preserve life. And God sent me before you to preserve your posterity on the earth. And to save your lives by a great deliverance. So now it was not you that sent me hither, but God: and He hath made me father to Pharaoh and lord of his entire house, and a ruler throughout all the land of Egypt" (Genesis 45:4-5; 7-80 KJV)

The devil meant it for Joseph's bad, but God had it in control all along. God is not sitting back waiting for the devil to do something in order for Him to respond to it. God is controlling every move the devil makes. The devil can do nothing except God allow him to do so. God is in control!

When we first read about Joseph in Genesis 37, he is telling on his brothers. His father gives him a coat with many colors. At the very least, anyone wearing such a garment would not be expected to do any real work. Joseph was a dreamer. He often shared the dreams with his brothers and his father. The dream of sheaves, the brothers' sheaves bowing down to Joseph's sheaf, incites his brothers' hatred. But the heavenly dream of the sun, moon and eleven stars bowing down to him, calls forth even his father's rebuke.

The brothers are off pasturing their flocks, and Jacob asked Joseph to go off and see how his brothers were. He would still be capable of telling, and of course he is wearing that fancy coat. "Here come this dreamer," the brothers said, and they determined to kill him. They stripped Joseph of his coat, threw him into a pit and planned to profit from him by selling him into slavery in Egypt. After dipping his coat in goat's blood, they gave it to Jacob, and persuaded him that Joseph was dead. Be careful who you tell your dreams to, they might try to kill you and your dreams. Now the great mystery unfolds. The spoiled brat managed to land on his feet and God's expected end for him began. Although it's in a world in which he knew nothing of, Joseph was operating in his destiny.

In the house of Potiphar, his new master in Egypt, he found Joseph worthy of responsibility. Joseph's good looks got him in trouble. Potiphar's wife wanted Joseph and set him up. Joseph's attractiveness brought on the false accusation of Potiphar's wife that landed him in prison. While in prison he was given responsibility for other prisoners; even there God is with him. If God be for you who can be against you? Yes, Joseph felt all the pain, but God was getting all the glory. Everything was working out for his good.

Your enemies are your blessing.

In jail Joseph helped his fellow prisoners with their dreams, and eventually helped Pharaoh with his. As a result, Pharaoh made him prime minister and gave him the responsibility for social affairs. Once he had worn a special coat with long sleeves; now he was wearing garments of linen and a gold necklace. God is in control! He will send you into the house of your enemy so that you can be blessed to be a blessing. Your enemies are your blessing even as Joseph's and Moses' enemies were their blessings. Now let me say this, "Everyone that God allows in your life is not for you to save. There are some that God allows to come in your life is to just bless you."

Back in Joseph's home land, Canaan, the famine had begun, and Joseph's family was determined to seek food in Egypt. Joseph's brothers went into Egypt and returned home confused because of Joseph's command; He kept Simeon hostage and told the brother to return with Benjamin.

Jacob is now in despair at the loss of Joseph, at the news that Simeon is being held hostage, and that now Benjamin is to be taken away. Both the brothers and Jacob are confused by the return of their money in their sacks and then by the appearance of Joseph's silver cup in their sacks.

Upon their return with Benjamin, the announcement came. Joseph is unable to control himself before the Egyptian court as he prepared to make himself known to his brothers. He identified himself, the brothers are bewildered, Joseph forgave his brothers and the whole family is thereby saved. Joseph said to his brothers, "And now do not be distressed, or angry with yourselves, because you sold me here; for God sent me before you to preserve life. Hurry and go up to my father and say to him, 'Thus says your son Joseph, God has made me lord of all Egypt; come down to me, do not delay.'"

I believe whole hearty that there are things God never intended for us to experience. But for reason beyond our control we experience them with much hurt and pain. God gets no glory out of our suffering. He gets glory from turning our suffering into blessings. Today it may feel bad, but tomorrow it will all be for your good. The Bible states that 'all things' are working together for my good. This plus that, plus that, is all working for me. God said it and that settles it. You may not have any control over where you are right now; however, you do have control over what you do while you are there.

Learning to Walk Again

I can recall a time, coming up as a child, when my mother was very sick. She had an issue of blood. Blood was so low in her body that my father had to raise her feet in bed so blood could flow to her head. She called her children to her bed to pray that God would spare the life of their mother.

The conditions were poor at home in the country, so dad moved mother to town, under the care of a church mother. There prayer was offered up daily for the recovering of her strength and health. Mother's one request to my father was, "Don't take me to the doctor; God is going to heal me." Faithfully my father worked with her request. Many turned against him because of it. Some even said that he wanted her to die. We were in a crisis.

All the strength left mother's body. She was bed ridden, unable to talk, unable to walk, unable to feed herself. In prayer the devil would often talk to my father saying, "What are you going to do when she die?" Dad would respond by saying, "What are you going to do when she live?"

Days went into weeks, weeks went into months. Little by little, strength began to return to mother's weak thin body. Her desire for food returned. Color returned to her face. One day while dad was away in the field she called me over to her bed side. Slowly she put her arm over my shoulder and pulled herself up from bed. "Take me to my husband", she said.

With one step in front of the other she learned to walk again. Over the floor, down the steps, down the dusty country road, we went, one step at a time. When dad looked up and saw us, joy filled his soul. All disappointments were gone. Sadness was made glad. The garment of heaviness was replaced with the garment of praise. One step at a time she began to live again. You too can live again, one step at a time.

What you are going through today is being made to bless you tomorrow. Your failures shall be your victory and your short comings shall be your success. The devil meant it for your bad, but God uses all things for our good. You cannot put scrambled eggs back inside its broken shell, but you surely can make a great omelet out of it.

CHAPTER XIV

Receiving What You Don't Deserve

How many times have you used the term, "Wish I had known that?" If you are as I am, I am sure you have used it many times in life. If I had only known, I wouldn't have bought that car. If I had only known, I would have kept my mouth shut. If I had only known, I wouldn't have married that man or woman. If I had only known! Well the truth is, you didn't know. It's for this reason one must always pray and seek God concerning relationships or for that matter, anything.

Some may disagree but, everyone who is married is not put together by God. There're some relationships we entered into upon our own. For an example, God had nothing to do with who you met in a dark night club or someone you had an unholy sex act with and married because of a pregnancy. Yes, I am sure if you had only known you would have done things differently. But the point is, "you didn't!"

I can recall a young lady who wanted a particular young man so badly. She did all she could to convince him to marry her, even to the point of giving birth to his child. Girls let me tell you now, "Having a baby for some boy is not the ticket to his heart". He will leave you and the baby! Not only will he leave you and the baby, he will have another girl while you are carrying his baby.

I am sure it was no less the same with King David in his affair with Bathsheba. To some the story of David and Bathsheba is a story of condemnation and to be true about it, it could be. However, it's actually, at least for those of us who are willing to admit it and have found ourselves in David's shoes, about grace, and restoration also. And for those of us who have experienced such failure, divorce, or other life's experience, I pray that this will be a word of hope, healing, and restoration that reminds us that God's plan is not to press and destroy us under His feet. God's plan is to heal and restore our relationship with Him. God wants you to live again. He is the God of a second chance, and He wants what's best for you.

Not being where you belong will always get you in trouble.

The story with David and Bathsheba begins in 2 Samuel 11 (KJV). "Then it happened in the spring, at the time when kings go out to battle, that David sent Joab and his servants with him and all Israel, and they destroyed the sons of Ammon and besieged Rabbi. But David stayed at Jerusalem. Now when evening came David arose from his bed and walked around on the roof of the king's palace, and from the roof he saw a woman bathing in her courtyard; and the woman was very beautiful in appearance. So David sent and inquired about the woman. And one said, "Is this not Bathsheba, the daughter of Elian, the wife of Uriah the Hittite?" David sent messengers and took her, and when she came to him, he lay with her; and when she had purified herself from her uncleanness, she returned to her house."

At the very beginning of this story, we find King David not being where he belonged. Not being where you belong will always get you in trouble. If David had been out in the battlefield, where the king was supposed to be, instead of hanging out on the rooftop of the palace, looking at naked women, this whole incident would have never happened. Some may say that David may have been tried and needed rest from wars. Other may say, "Every man needs a break." In any case, David wasn't where he was support to be. In life you will discover, if you will admit it, that this is often the first step of an out of control situation that will lead to a crash and death. Whenever you are 'out of place', you cause everything around you to be 'misplaced', and when this happen you can go 'no place.' When you add it all up, out of place plus misplaced equal going no place.

Not doing what you should do will always get you in trouble.

Let me point out here that, when viewed through the eyes of most church people, it's easy to say that Bathsheba shared in David's sin as a willing partaker, or if nothing else, she had no business bathing where the King could see her. The point still is, David was out of place! And beside in those days, the King was the one who was in total control. He had absolute authority. If Bathsheba was summoned by the King to come to his palace, then she came to the palace or risked being killed for rejecting the King's order.

Personally, I believe that Bathsheba's bathing was not in a public place, but probably behind a wall. Some may say, "She was in the wrong place at the wrong time." The point made is, Bathsheba was in her right place, and David was out of place. She had no idea that she would be seen. She was in her right place, at home. And besides, the King was supposed to be out in the battlefield with 'her' husband.

Now let me also point out that David didn't set out to commit a dangerous sin act. As being born again believers we seldom do; however, it does happen. When first asked about Bathsheba, David didn't know her identity or whether or not she was married. Being unmarried, David would have been quite proper in pursuing her as a wife, and his asking about her would not have been improper. By the time David learned that she was married, he had already let his lust over take him. Lust can do that to any person, even you, if you allow it to burn long enough. That's why the Bible said, "Run from youthful lust", meaning "Run before it gets to big to stop." You have to know which head to follow.

It would appear that David's intention was never to take Bathsheba as a wife but to just plain have sex with her. David had no plans on a long-term affair, just a one-night sexual affair with a good-looking-fine woman. But as usual, sin had its consequences.

149

I am reminded of the story of a lovely woman who worked in the downtown area of Milwaukee. She was in management of a well-known company and held a good position in the company. Often the company would send her off on business trips where she stayed for several days. Upon one of her trips, out of the city, she met a handsome young man who asked her out for dinner. Being a born again believer she declined.

The young man was very persistent in obtaining a date, and besides he was tall, dark, and handsome. While in the city, daily he would send her flowers and candy to sway her his way. After being overwhelmed with gifts, on the last night in the city, the young lady gave in to his desires. Dinner was nice, at the finest of restaurant.

The devil will put someone in your path today to over throw you tomorrow

Afterward she was invited to his hotel room for an evening of soft music. Without planning and before she knew it, she found herself in a passionate sex act.

Upon leaving the next day, the young man met her at the airport with another going away gift; she was impressed. He asked if she would wait and open it in flight home on the plane. Once in flight she opened the gift and to her surprise it was a strange gift. Upon opening the gift she discovered a small coffin with a black rose inside with a note attached. The note read, "Welcome to the world of AIDS." If I had only known.

The story of David and Bathsheba, goes on to tell us that, Bathsheba conceived. Oops, wasn't expecting that. David hadn't planned on this. Have you ever heard the term, "What you don't know can't hurt you?" That's a false statement. What this young woman didn't know caused her everything. In most cases when such a statement is made, someone is trying to avoid knowledge about particular things. They feel that by not knowing, they are protecting themselves, mainly their feelings, or by not knowing they are not held responsible. However, in reality, what you don't know can cost you everything, even your life.

Imagine traveling down a long dark road. Fifty miles ahead there's a bridge out. The last exit for exiting the road is two miles ahead before the bridge. Because of your lack of knowledge concerning the bridge, you pass the last exit. Forty-eight miles later you come upon the out bridge. Because of the darkness, no warning, and no knowledge, you drive off the edge and are badly injured. Why? Because you didn't know.

The odds were against you; it was a dark road, you couldn't see where you were going, no one had gone before you to inform you of the condition ahead, and there were no warning sign. This is the perfect condition for destruction. It's like playing the lottery and taking a chance on your life's earnings, when the odd for you of winning is totally against you. The sad thing about the situation on the dark road is this; your lack of knowledge didn't stop you from dealing with the consequences of not knowing. The consequences still happened! The young lady not knowing, didn't stop her from dealing with the consequences of AIDS.

Trapped By the Trapper

Growing up in the country in Mississippi, my Indian grandfather taught me a thing or two about trapping. The success of being a great trapper is to make the trap not appear as a trap. You do this by placing the trap in the path where animals travel and cover it with leaves and dirt from the path, making it giving the impression of being like the path. By not being able to know the difference, the animal steps in the trap and is caught. If I had only known. God said we are destroyed because we don't know.

The enemy studies the path we travel. He knows our weaknesses and strengths. He knows what we desire, want, and need. Be careful, what you desire could become your trap. The devil will plant something or someone in your life today that will overthrow you tomorrow. Like an old wise trapper, he plans his trap for you. It appears good and nice on the outside; however, it's a cover-up. It's not what it appears to be. Run quickly from youthful lusts! RUN!

The statement "If I had only known" indicates that one is void of knowledge or facts about a particular thing or situation. In other words what we are saying is, "I didn't know"; therefore, if I had only known means, if I only had facts or information that is certain, or that which is proven to be true. In layman terms the statement is saying, "If I had only had the facts or knowledge of what was ahead." If only David had known the trouble that lying with Bathsheba would bring. If only this young lady had known. Maybe, just maybe, they would have taken another path.

The Path We Take

Life is a trip. We travel this road daily into areas we have never gone before; feeling our way through, making major life's changing decisions in hope of having a good outcome. Allow me to say, "Life is too precious, odds are against you and circumstances are too dangerous for you to be traveling the long dark highway of life without sight. You need to see where you are going." The rule for driving in darkness is, "Never over drive your headlights." In plain English it means: Never drive faster than what you can see ahead of you without being able to make a stop if need be.

Sight is knowledge. Have you ever said, "I see it now?" Meaning I understand now, or have you ever said, "I was in the dark on that?" Meaning, I didn't know. Therefore, sight would mean knowledge and dark would mean a lack of or void of knowledge. Knowledge is information in mind; it is general awareness or possession of information, facts, ideas, truths, or principles. Therefore 'knowledge' would be specific information at hand, of a particular situation or fact.

When one has knowledge they 'know' what the outcome is ahead of time. Know is to be certain about something by having a thorough understanding of it through experience or study. When one knows something they can perceive the difference or distinction between things or people. Example: I know that if I save $5.00 each day for seven days, I will have $35.00. I know, 'now" what I will have 'before' the seven days. It's called 'foreknowledge.

Foreknowledge gives you sight of the end now.

Foreknowledge is knowledge of something 'before' it happens. This is knowledge or awareness that something is going to happen, either from information that has been acquired, or by prophetic means. I have foreknowledge of what I will have on the seventh day today, because I have knowledge on what $5.00 for seven days will be. I obtained this knowledge through studying. Not only do I have knowledge of it, I can also tell you what you will or what you will not have by saving $5.00 for seven days or by not saving $5.00 for seven days. God has allowed others before us, traveling the same road we now travel, that we may know what lies ahead. It is for sure a true statement, "A hard head will always lead to a soft behind."

Take Responsibility

If only I could turn back the hands of time. How many times have we said this? However, it's impossible to turn back the hands of time. Yesterday is over! No doubt David said, "If only I could go back in time, I would be where I belong; in the battlefield with my men."

It does matter how much we wish or desire for it to be, it's not going to happen. Since one can't go back in time, what is one to do in a situation where they wish they hadn't done something or had done things differently? Well, you have to take responsibility for what you've done. This is one of the hardest things to face. I have learned that what one fears the most is not so much the responsibility, but the consequence. Responsibility is standing up to and taking the blame for something. Consequence on the other hand is the outcome for the responsibility.

There's no right in wrong!

David had sinned, and as usual, there's an outcome to sin, and David had to face it. We all have to face our sins! Not knowing doesn't exempt you from the consequences. Not knowing the law doesn't exempt you from the law. David didn't know that Bathsheba would get pregnant; however, he did know that sex could get a woman pregnant. Bathsheba wasn't David first woman!

David demonstrated that he was just like the rest of us. He went with his first instinct; he tried to cover up his sin and shift the responsibility to someone else instead of taking ownership of his action. This goes all the way back to the fall of man when God confronted Adam in the garden about his sins. Instead of Adam admitting his sins and taking responsibility he shifted the responsibility by saying, "It's the woman to blame. It's her fault!" In reality Adam was saying, "God, it's really your fault. You gave me the woman. If you hadn't given me this woman I wouldn't be in this situation." We are all like that. David was no different; he tried to cover his sin.

Often times, men and women, boys and girls try to cover their sin act of sex outside of marriage, now expecting a child, by getting married. First of all the purpose of the marriage is wrong. Not because of love for each other, but to cover the expecting of the child. Some may say, "Well that's the best thing for them to do." The best thing is not always the right thing. The right thing was to not have sex outside of marriage. Getting married doesn't turn wrong into right. You can't make wrong right! There's no right in wrong.

Uriah, Bathsheba's husband, was a faithful warrior who was out on the battlefield; the same battlefield where David should have been. David called Uriah in from the battle, pretending to reward him for being faithful. Afterward he told Uriah to go home, assuming that Uriah would go and have sex with Bathsheba, after all, he had been away for a period of time. After sex with Bathsheba, Uriah would think that the baby was his, and David's sin would be covered.

The one thing that David didn't think of in his plan was Uriah's faithfulness and loyalty. He would not go home and enjoy the pleasures of his wife when his fellow-soldiers were camping out in the battlefield. Uriah was a man's man. David even tried getting him drunk, but Uriah's sense of duty and honor was strong enough to overcome all of David's tricks. Finally, David got desperate, and like most desperate men, David did something stupid. Have you ever done something stupid? Don't let your desperation causes you to do something stupid and add to the problem you already have. Don't be a fool twice.

Verse 14-17 "Now in the morning David wrote a letter to Joab and sent it by the hand of Uriah. He had written in the letter, saying, "Place Uriah in the front line of the fiercest battle and withdraw from him, so that he may be struck down and die." So it was as Joab kept watch on the city, that he put Uriah at the place where he knew there were valiant men. The men of the city went out and fought against Joab, and some of the people among David's servants fell; and Uriah the Hittite also died.""

To sin could cause the lives of many.

David sent word to the leader of his army, and told him to put Uriah in a place where he would be killed. What you don't know can kill you. Although he did not know why the king had ordered Uriah's death, the leader obeyed David's command, probably thinking that the king had good reason for it, and besides who would question the king's order. It could have cost him his life.

The only way that he could trick a seasoned warrior like Uriah was to cause several other good men to die with him. As sad as it many sound, covering up your sins are often like that, a lot of innocent people get hurt while we are trying to hide the truth. It would have been best for David to have been in his place of operation from the beginning. Lives would have been spared and David's family would have had the blessing of God upon them instead of a curse.

Bathsheba hears the news of her husband's death and mourned for him. Then, as a sign of an understanding king, David takes Bathsheba in and made her one of his wives. What a cover-up! David had sex with Uriah's wife, gets her pregnant, tries to get her husband to have sex with her so he can think it's his, he doesn't, so David had him killed and married the man's wife as if he cares about her condition. In the eyes of all, King David appeared to be supportive. But in secret it was a cover-up. David thought the whole incident was covered. The only living person who knew the entire truth and could testify against him was Bathsheba, and now she was his wife.

There's one thing of importance about covering sin. You may fool and hid things from people; howbeit, you can never cover and hid things from God. You can rest assured; your sins will always find you out.

Set Up By God

Proverbs 6:2 (KJV) Thou art snared with the words of thy mouth, thou art taken with the words of thy mouth.

The word snared means to trap. Solomon, the son of King David, later wrote about the entrapment of his father's words in the above scripture. David was trapped by what he said. Believe it or not, David was setup by God and serve notice on this, "God will set you up." He will set you up to bless you and He will also set you up to bring you down. When one is setup they don't know it.

A setup is a carefully thought out plan of action to bring about a desired result by putting a person in a position where they think it's for one reason, when in reality the plan is all together designed for something totally different. In layman terms it's tricking a person into doing what one desires. Trick is a cunning deception: a cunning action or plan that is intended to deceive someone by intentionally leading them away from the truth.

The words of King David were law. Whatever he decreed was established and carried out. God setup David with his own words. On that I say to you, "Be careful what you say because you could be passing sentence on yourself.

2 Samuel 12:1-6 (KJV) "Then the LORD sent Nathan to David. And he came to him and said, "There were two men in one city, the one rich and the other poor. The rich man had a great many flocks and herds. But the poor man had nothing except one little ewe lamb which he bought and nourished. And it grew up together with him and his children. It would eat of his bread and drink of his cup and lie in his bosom, and was like a daughter to him. Now a traveler came to the rich man, and he was unwilling to take from his own flock or his own herd, to prepare for the wayfarer who had come to him; rather he took the poor man's ewe lamb and prepared it for the man who had come to him." Then David's anger

burned greatly against the man, and he said to Nathan, "As the LORD lives, surely the man who has done this deserves to die. He must make restitution for the lamb fourfold, because he did this thing and had no compassion."

Nathan's story was about what David had done, and had covered it up so skillfully. This should remind us that, no matter how hard we try, we can't hide from God. We're much better off if we're just honest with Him up front, it's not like He doesn't already know. God is all seeing and all knowing, and He said, "Be sure, your sins will find you out."

God set David up through Nathan the prophet, and David took the bait. It never ceases to amaze me that though a person can sin, their office of operation is still anointed. David still had an anointing for compassion, even though he had ignored it in his own life. David, as king, had authority to pronounce judgment on such criminals, and that's exactly what he did, not realizing that he was pronouncing his own judgment: the death penalty. Afterward Nathan told David the meaning of the story.

God is bigger and smarter than we are. There's nothing hidden from Him. Nathan told David exactly what he had done, and pronounced God's judgment on the king. It's important to understand Nathan's situation. He risked his life by bringing this accusation before the king. The king had the sole power of authority; he could have told one of the guards to kill Nathan on the spot. He could have denied his sin, and argued with Nathan (and with God). He could have rebelled against them and continued in his denial. The choice was David's to make. He could have continued in denial, with words such as "I did NOT have sex with that woman." Instead, David came face-to-face with himself and made the most important statement of his life. "Then David said to Nathan, "I have sinned against the LORD." (2 Samuel 12:13 KJV)

The Lord said that if we confess our sins He is just and faithful to forgive us and to cleanse us from all unrighteous. Forgiveness began with taking responsibility. There has to be no blame-shifting, no excuses, and no double-talking. You have to see your situation clearly, and deal with it boldly. When this happens, you can find God's mercy.

David confessed his sin. Now it would have been fully justified if God had carried out the sentence pronounced upon David by his own judgment. When we are truly honest with God, we will always find His mercy and grace.

And Nathan said to David, "The LORD also has taken away your sin; you shall not die." (2 Samuel 12:13 KJV)

David got what he did not desire, grace.

CHAPTER XV

Man of Still

A little boy got himself in trouble with his mother as little boys often do and he was firmly told to sit down and be quiet. The little fellow had a stubborn streak and totally refused to have a seat. His mother became even more firm and told him to sit down before he got into more trouble than he was already in. Half-heartedly, he plopped down in the chair, looked up at his mother and whispered, "Ok, on the outside I'm sitting down, but on the inside I'm still standing!"

Acts 19:11-16 (KJV) "God did extraordinary miracles through Paul, so that even handkerchiefs and aprons that had touched him were taken to the sick, and their illnesses were cured and the evil spirits left them. Some Jews who went around driving out evil spirits tried to invoke the name of the Lord Jesus over those who were demon-possessed. They would say, "In the name of Jesus, whom Paul preaches, I command you to come out." Seven sons of Sceva, a Jewish chief priest, were doing this. One day the evil spirit answered them, "Jesus I know, and I know about Paul, but who are you?" Then the man who had the evil spirit jumped on them and overpowered them all. He gave them such a beating that they ran out of the house naked and bleeding."

Jesus is the best thing that ever happened to me.

It is of a true; I've had my shares of life's ups and downs. Some downs have been so low I could have sat on a dine and swung my legs. However, through all of my life's ups and down, I can say of a true, "Jesus is the best thing that ever happened to me."

When you are going through your lows and downs, it is extremely important to know who you are in Christ. If a person were locked in a jail cell for years, and someone came and unlocked the cell door for them, and they did not know that the door was unlocked, the freedom that they had obtained would be of no effect.

As children of God, when we accept Christ and receive His Spirit, we have the power of God dwelling inside of us, but if we don't know that we have this power it is of no effect. There is much power inside of you to overcome the aftermath of all trials and pains that have come into your life. "Greater is He that is within you than he that is in the world." (1 John 4:4 KJV)

Greater simply means more. The One who is more than enough is in the inside of you. If you are in Christ Jesus, the Holy Spirit, the One who is more, is on the inside of you. Because of this we have overcoming power.

This should be the heart cry of every believer. The greater One lives within me. It is because of the greater One that lives within me, I am victorious. It is because of the greater One that lives within me that I am successful. It is because of the greater One that dwells within me, causes me to triumph in every circumstance of life. Some people would say this is bragging. If it's bragging, it's certainly isn't bragging on me, it's bragging on God and His ability. I am not saying what I can do but what God in me can and is doing.

We should make it a habit to continually declare that the greater One makes us victorious. When we declare this, we are lining our words up with God's words. We are giving God a place to work in our lives when we speak what He has told us to speak. This is not presumption it is obedience to His Word. Presumption is to assume something, and I am not talking about that at all. I am talking about acting on knowledge. I am acting on what I know to be true and declaring it to be so.

In the opening scripture there were a group of men conducting an exorcism to drive demons out of an individual. They believed that by simply doing so saying the name of Jesus; they had the power of Jesus. They had seen and heard Paul do these things. Instead they found themselves running from the house naked and wounded.

The demons knew Jesus. They had heard of Paul probably from Satan himself. But the demons didn't recognize them because these men weren't in the family of God. Scripture teaches us, if we resist the devil by faith in Christ, he will flee from us; but if we think we can resist him by just using Jesus' name, as a spell or charm, Satan will prevail against us as he did these seven men.

Only those who are in the family of God have the right to use the Name of Jesus.

If we are true followers of God and obedient to His word, we will become a threat to the kingdom of darkness. Therefore, Satan will assign more demons to pursue and try to overthrow us.

Are you a threat to the kingdom of darkness? If Satan and his demons were to evaluate you what would they say when your name is called? Would they say that you are one of their most feared enemies and they needed to keep many demons harassing and opposing you? Or would they say, "This person poses no threat to our activities. Leave him alone".

In my book, I Must Be from Another Planet, I wrote about how God showed me that demons in hell took counsel among themselves on how to stop me. When you are a treat to the kingdom of darkness, hell will take counsel on you! If you truly believe that you are at war against rulers and principalities that cannot be seen, then you must realize that their instruction is to hinder you at any cost and stop you from walking in the fullness of God. However, "Greater is He that is in you, than he that is in the world" (1 John. 4:4b KJV).

Chosen by God

Isaiah chapter 48 (KJV) says: "See, I have tested you in the furnace of affliction. For my own sake, for my own sake, I do this ...."

We have been chosen by God to be in His family. Wow, that's great; to serve Him, yes; to praise Him, of course; but to suffer in the furnace of affliction? Yes! No one likes being afflicted, but it's true. But there is a wonderful comfort even in this, because when God chooses us to suffer, it is for His own sake, and he repeats it again, "for My own sake, I do this."

Acts 9:10-15 (KJV) "Now there was a disciple at Damascus named Ananias; and the Lord said to him in a vision, "Ananias." And he said, "Here I am, Lord." And the Lord said to him, "Get up and go to the street called Straight, and inquire at the house of Judas for a man from Tarsus named Saul, for he is praying, and he has seen in a vision a man named Ananias come in and lay his hands on him, so that he might regain his sight." But Ananias answered, "Lord, I have heard from many about this man, how much harm he did to Your saints at Jerusalem; and here he has authority from the chief priests to bind all who call on Your name. But the Lord said to him, "Go, for he is a chosen instrument of Mine, to bear My name before the Gentiles and kings and the sons of Israel; for I will show him how much he must suffer for My name's sake."

In the above verses is where I found divine revelation into the eternal counsel of God. God revealed to Ananias that Saul was His "chosen instrument" (Acts 9:15 KJV). The word chosen here means "to select for one's own purpose". God chooses or elects those to serve Him for purpose. Election is always the free choice of God, based on His sovereignty, and never based of the worthiness of the individual. God chose you because He wants to.

God chose Saul, not because he was sweet and lovely and doing all the right things; rather, the Lord chose Saul in order to demonstrate His grace, His love and His power. As the "chosen instrument" of the Lord, Saul was to carry the Lord's name "before the Gentiles and kings and the sons of Israel". Thank God for His sovereign grace!

God did not select me nor you because we were so sweet, so lovely and doing all the right things either. When God saved me I was main lining heroin in my body. What were you doing? Even as it was with Saul, God chose me, and you, to demonstrate His grace, His love and His power.

Not every Christian will suffer for their faith. There are Christians whom the Lord has blessed with a life of peace and prosperity. However, when looking through Scripture as well as through the history of my life, suffering is more the norm rather than the exception. For the Christian, joy is not found in the absence of suffering, but in doing God's will and being found pleasing in His sight, for His sake.

She Called Me Out

I will never forget the day, time and place when she called me out, the prophetess of God. "Milton", she said, "The Lord said your name will be known throughout the portholes of hell." Praises went up with a blast as I received the word that fell from the prophetess of God's mouth. My name will be known throughout the portholes of hell. The devil is going to know me just like he knew Jesus and Paul! What a place for your name to be known, hell. Not on earth, and not in heaven, but throughout the portholes of hell. What an assignment!

I praised God as I thought; the devil is in trouble now. I'm going to be casting out demons, kicking devils butts, healing the sick, raising the dead. The blind will see, the lame will walk, and the devil and all of hell will know Apostle Milton Adams by name. Expecting agreement from the prophetess, I asked, "How will he know me? By what wonderful work will hell know me?"

Allow me to say that whatever God does for you and me is without importance on our part and by pure grace on His part, and it is done for a purpose. God never gives to or benefits His children just for our own selfish ends. Don't think it unusual if you find yourself fighting major battles as you become more obedient to the Father. God desires for each of us to become a feared enemy of hell: however, your name cannot be known in hell without going through hell.

Going Thru Hell

Jesus told us in John 16:33, (KJV) "I have told you these things, so that in Me you may have peace. In this world you will have trouble. But take heart! I have overcome the world." Jesus is saying, "In this world you are going to go thru hell.

In order to not offend my church brothers and sisters and for sure to my church Elders, Bishops and Apostles, I want to establish for you what the term "Going through Hell" means. In my research for this book I discovered that the phase, "Going through hell" means, to have a very unpleasant troubling experience that lasts for a long period of time. In layman terms it simply means, "Having trouble".

Jesus didn't say, "You might have trouble." Jesus didn't say, "You might go through hell." Jesus didn't say, "You will only have trouble, or only go through hell, when you're out of God's will." Jesus said, "In this world you WILL have trouble." Will indicate the certainty and unavoidability of something happening. Jesus is clear on the point that we will all go through hell. I want you to know that, "If you're going through hell right now I have some good news for you; you're going through it, not staying in it.

As long as you are "Going Through" it tells me that you haven't taken up resident there. Through means that you are passing from one side or from one end of something to the other side or end of it. Through means from the beginning until the end and conclusion of it. Through means the completion of, or have finished something. Through don't mean stopping or getting stuck in the middle of something. Through mean proceeding or extending from one side or one end of something to the other or through something and beyond it and be finished with it! You may be going through; however, you are not stuck in it.

Don't Stop, Keep Going

During a bad tornado season, a lady who had lost everything after a tornado hit her home said, "I have lost everything; but I've got my life. I've never been through nothing like this before, but thank God I'm on the other side of it." It's one thing to go through an overwhelming, upsetting, crushing experience; however, it's another thing to get to the other side. This woman was saying, "I've been through hell but I am now on the other side of my hell experience". The number one rule for going through hell is, "Don't stop, and keep going". If you keep going you won't get stuck in the middle!

There's a place between the beginning and the end. That place where we realize what God has promised and yet we have not apprehended what God has promised. You are in the church. You have walked with God like you should, but you have not yet apprehended. You have given up some things expecting and believing God for some things but have not yet received those things. You are caught in the middle. Middle means you are located somewhere between the start and finish, operating in an intermediate position. Operating in the middle.

In the middle is in a place where you can't go back to the things that are behind you and you are now reaching forth unto those things that are before you, but for some reason, known or unknown to you, you haven't grasped hold of those things yet. As a matter of fact you can't go back because your Going Back Bridge is burnt. What was back is no longer there. There were times in life when I would have gone back if my Going Back Bridge was there. You are not where you used to be and you are not where you are going or where you are destined to be. You are here in this intermediate place.

Being stuck in the middle, smack dab in the middle sometimes is the best place to be to see God do His thing, if you are stuck in the middle with Him. Now, the question I want to ask you is, "What are you going to do while you are stuck? In other words, you are in this place, now what? What are you going to do next? One thing for sure, this I speak from experience and revelation, "If you don't move forward you will be stuck in nowhere being a damn soul.

Damn Soul

When I speak of a "damn soul", I am reminded of the story which revealed the meaning of the Jack-O- Lantern. The tale states that Jack was the town drunk that tricked the devil up a tree and wouldn't let him down. Upon the death of Jack the tale said he went to heaven; however St Peter met him at the Pearly Gates and told Jack there was no room for him. So he sent him to hell. When he made it to the gates of hell the devil met him there and said, "Because of what you did to me you can't come in". Jack was casted out into a place of wondering. He became a damn soul, stuck in no place.

Face to Face

The prophetess stood before me, face to face, with tears in her eyes and brokenness in her heart. She said to me, "Milton, when the rubbish, trash, waste and ruin are removed from over and around you, the enemy will find you still standing; a man of still. Still standing, still going strong, still faithful and still saved!

"Still standing" tells me that I will be hit with mighty blows from the enemy. Blows that could take you out. If you are seeking to fully follow the Lord, you can expect to be hit by the enemy with great persecution. God permits persecution to come for three reasons. First, for your sake; because it makes us stronger and draws us closer to Him. Secondly, for His sake. To express to hell our love for Him even as it was for Paul. Thirdly, for the sake of others. These are the times that God reveals His power; in our persecution to deliver others. Our message becomes fruitful when it is born out of obedience and suffering for His name because as testimonies, they become gifts that can be used for God's purpose to build bridges for others to be able to cross, to bring the unsaved to Christ.

"When the rubbish, trash, waste and ruin are removed from over and around you, the enemy will find you still standing." This prophecy tells me that I was about to go thru hell. Everything that was over me and around me was about to collapse. That which I had built, that which I lived for, that which I believed and trusted, that which I had dreamed was all going to collapse and no one was going to be there in the end but me; howbeit, the prophecy also said, "You shall still be standing!"

You are going to go through, but you shall come out! "The enemy will find you still standing", lets me know that after my going through, the enemy will still be there. He shall "find me" beneath what I have been going through, what he has tried to overthrow me with. I will still be standing; a man of still. I know that some of you are going through the greatest fire of your life, and it's the kind that hurts, and the kind that makes you cry, and I know it's going to sound crazy, but what you ought to be doing is praising God, that you made it through the fire.

There are many other people that never made it to the fire; there are other people that died at the door. Do you understand what I'm saying? It's a miracle that you made it this far, by all rights you shouldn't be here. You shouldn't have lived through that car wreck. Others died you didn't! You shouldn't have live through that bad relationship. Others lost their mind. Some took their life, but praise God you made it and is still standing. As a matter of fact you know it's a miracle that you are not in a mental institution somewhere. Other people have gone through a lot less than what you went through and they lost their minds, they went off the deep end. But God...

"But" always x's out what was before it. But is always greater than what previously was before it. When "But God" is viewed in relation to the challenges of life it stands totally opposed to the negative roar of the world. "But God" is what up is to down. "But God" is what life is to death; what in is to out. The world says no, "But, God" says yes! The world says can't, "But, God" says can! The world says won't: "But, God" says will! The world says stop, "But, God" says go! The world says don't, "But, God" says do!

The world says defeat, "But, God" says victory! "But, God" climbs the highest mountain; crosses the darkest valley; and sings songs of victory in the midnight hour! "But, God" exclaims, "I'm going to the enemy's camp and I'll take back what he stole from me!" "But, God" is courageous, confident and conclusive!" Brothers and sisters you have to realize that I'm speaking to you this evening from God's perspective!

What are you trying to tell me Apostle? I'm trying to tell you that you ought to be praising God that you made it to the fire, and through the fire. There are others that died at the door of their going through but God. They died where your miracle began.

I know, nobody expected for you to make it, but here you are alive, in your right mind, serving God, filled with the Holy Ghost and power. You don't have time to complain. You made it to the fire and through the fire. You could have died at the door, you could have died in that car wreck, you could have died of a drug overdose, you could be serving life in prison, and you could have lost your mind, But God... He had his hand on you! I don't know about you, but I wasn't the strongest one, I wasn't the smartest one, I wasn't the most popular one, I wasn't the one expected to make it, but I made it, and there's no other explanation but God.

You Are Coming Out

I want to prophesy to you and declare to you, "God wouldn't bring you to it if He wasn't going to bring you through it. Something good is going to come out of what you going through. You are going to make it, and you are not going to burn up in the fire. You are coming out! You might come out crawling on your hands and knees, but you are coming out! You might come out all beat up, you might come out broke busted and disgusted; howbeit, you are coming out!"

I cannot promise you that you will come out with everything you started with, but you will come out! I watch as solider come home from war. Those who are on the frontline, in the war zone, in the heat of the battle often come back with less than what they went in with. Some come back with missing body parts. They lose in the battle but they win in the war! The battle takes away from you. I can testify that the battle can cause you to lose body parts. In the battle you can lose wife, husband, sisters, brothers, sons and daughters. The battle can even take your sight and vision away from you. The battle takes things away from you!

I know we're faith people and I don't want to be negative, but I must say, "The battle can even knock you down and knock you out." If you be honest and tell the truth, you have been knocked down a time or two. The fact is sometimes the devil will hit you with something you never expected and it knocks the wind out of you and you find yourself lying on the ground saying what happened.

When you come out of this, your body may display the marks of battle, but your spirit will wear the sign of victory. You will come out blessed! You will come out delivered! When you come out sadness might be on your face, but you will come out with joy, peace and a greater anointing than you've ever had in your life.

Amaze Your Enemy

God spoke to me and said, "I'm going to amaze you". When God amaze you, you will amaze your enemies. Amaze means to overwhelm with surprise or sudden wonder; astonish greatly; to shock! When you come out you are going to shock your enemies. They never thought you would come back. They never thought you would make it through.

I'm amazing the devil who thought he had me; I'm amazing the devil and people who thought because they hurt me and made me cry it was over. It ain't over till God says it over and I haven't heard no fat lady sing. I'm amazing my enemies, the ones who saw me go into the fire, added to the fire, and took pleasure in it. The ones who said I'd never make it. The ones who said I'd burn up in the fire. The ones who said I'll go back to drugs and the drugs would kill me. The ones who prophesy I'll die young. The ones who said I'll lose my mind. But I'm still here. Why? Because I'm a man of still. And guess what, "I'm amazing myself."

Yes, I went through hell but I'm still standing. Yes, the devil hit me hard, and I went down and it hurt and I cried for a while, but I'm still standing. And I have a news flash for the devil, I'm up again, and I'm on my feet again, and I'm still standing. Out of all the things I been through, I still have joy. I have been hurt, but I'm still standing. I've been misunderstood, but I'm still standing. The devil knocked me off my feet, but I'm up again and I'm still standing.

I got my joy back, I got my peace back, I got my swag back, I got my dance back, and I got my praise back. I've got my faith and ministry back. And if the devil thought I was a problem before, he ain't seen trouble yet because while I was in the battle, I was working on my praise. While I was in the battle I was working on my shout. While I was in the battle I was working on my dance. It might be a one leg, one armed, and half a vision dance, but it's a dance of victory, and guess what, I'm still standing because I am a man of still!

Someone has said that "If you don't stand for something, you will fall for anything." That statement is also true in a spiritual sense. If a person does not have an anchor for their soul, they will be swept away with the tide of life.

Build your life on a foundation of obedience to God's Word so that you will ride out the storms in your life. The Bible says that, "When the storm has swept by, the wicked are gone, but the righteous stand firm forever!" (Proverbs 10:25 KJV).

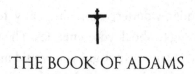

CHAPTER XVI

Broken But Usable

Leviticus 21:16-23 (KJV) "16. The LORD said to Moses, 17. "Say to Aaron: (Aaron is Moses blood brother, both from the Levi tribe)"For the generations to come none of your descendants who has a defect may come near to offer the food of his God. 18. No man who has any defect may come near: no man who is blind or lame, disfigured or deformed; 19. No man with a crippled foot or hand, 20. Or who is hunchbacked or dwarfed, or who has any eye defect, or who has rotten or running sores or damaged testicles. 21. No descendant of Aaron the priest who has any defect is to come near to present the offerings made to the LORD by fire. He has a defect; he must not come near to offer the food of his God. 22. He may eat the most holy food of his God, as well as the holy food; 23. Yet because of his defect, (Because he's not perfect) he must not go near the curtain or approach the altar, and so desecrate my sanctuary. I am the LORD, who makes them holy".

A young boy with the capacity to do great art work was creating a masterpiece in his art class when he accidentally knocked over a container of paint on his masterpiece. It was ruined. Heartbroken and with tears running down his face, he approached his instructor saying, "I've accidentally spilled paint on my masterpiece and now it's ruined forever". The instructor looked the heartbroken boy in his eyes and said, "Its ok, you can begin again". Though your masterpiece is ruined forever, never to be restored, never to be seen, never to reach the value and worth as to what it could have become, its ok, you can begin again. You are still in the art class!

Jeremiah 18:1-4 (KJV) The word which came to Jeremiah from the Lord, saying, Arise, and go down to the potter's house, and there I will cause thee to hear my words. Then I went down to the potter's house, and, behold, he wrought a work on the wheels. And the vessel that he made of clay was marred in the hand of the potter: so he made it again another vessel, as seemed good to the potter to make it.

In the above verses, God commanded Jeremiah the prophet to arise, and go down to the potter's house, and there He would cause Jeremiah to hear His words. Jeremiah goes to the potter's house and when he gets there the potter is fashioning a work on the wheel. The potter is making a vessel.

There watching the potter work the clay in fashioning the vessel, God speaks to Jeremiah through the work of the potter. Isn't it amazing how God speaks to us? In the making of the vessel, after going through all the processes of hand selecting the right clay, throwing it on the wheel, beating it so it can form to his hand, taking out all the pebbles, shaping the clay into the vessel he desired, the Bible said in verse 4 "And the vessel that he made of clay was marred in the hand of the potter". Meaning, that while in his hands, the vessel that HE, the POTTER was making became disfigured, messed up, and had a defect in it, while it was in the making process. In the making process the vessel became messed up "before" it was a finished creation.

How many of us had messed up before God got through with us? While we was yet in the making process, while we were still in His hands, while we were still in the church, singing on the praise team or preaching from the pulpit, we messed up. Sound like church folks to me. Jeremiah stated that once discovered that the vessel in making had a defect the potter did an amazing thing. Instead of throwing it away or aborting it, he decided, by his own choice, to make it again another vessel as seemed good to the potter to make.

There's so much here to review. After the fact it was messed up, the potter begin again, to make it again, another vessel. "He made it..." Made here means that the Potter decided to form it in a different place using a different process. The potter knew that the same thing beget the same result. I was told that insanity was doing the same thing expecting a different result. In order to get a different result, the potter had to take it out of the place where he ordinarily made it first, the place which caused the mess up. He relocated it and formed it through a different process of making. Here's the kicker here, you thought the first place and the first process was tough and hot, wait till you are made again.

There are many that the Lord is removing and relocating as it was with Abraham. God is saying, "Leave your father's house. Leave family members. Relocate to a new place where I will show you. If you remain you will never change."

Doing the same thing get the same result

He made it "again". Again means that the potter made it, another time, once more, a second time. Gave it a second chance. He is the God of a second chance. Glory! Howbeit, second chance doesn't mean that second, once more chance or another time is easier.

One must realize that if one messed up in the first process and God decides to make you over again, the second process will be greater. The second process will be harder, not easier. The pressing will be greater. The beating will be greater. The heat will be greater. But you can shout right now, because your outcome will also be greater. Your blessing will be greater and most of all you will be greater with a greater anointing. I am a second time, one more chance, another time vessel. Messed up but still anointed!

Double Work, Double Time

Now, let's look at this from the potter's point of view. He's doing double work, double time in order to get the vessel to the place where he can use it. Double work means, double beating, double pressing, double amount of time on the wheel. The potter is in double time mode, putting twice amount of time in you. Double also means greater. If God put double time in you, it comes with double pay. You will have to pay for the Master's double time. You are a double time vessel. Why? Because you refuse to be fashioned into what God had in mind for you during the first process. It was God's first plan for you to be a choir boy.

Since you refuse to form to your first calling, God's mandate is still on your life. Too much is invested in you. God has put too much time in you to just let you go. Now, here's revelation. Double work on you means you will now be an Apostle, or Pastor instead of a choir boy. An Apostle? A Pastor? Glory! Don't shout right now because it takes more to be an Apostle or Pastor than a choir boy. With the Apostle's calling is double trouble because He put double work in you. By the time He's finished with you, you will wish you were a choir boy.

Here's the kicker. About 90% of the time, when making a vessel on the potter's wheel, the vessel turns out fine the first time. It forms willingly to the making of the potter. But there's that 10% of us who will not form willingly and properly to the Master's hand. We rebel and mess up, while still in the Master's hands, before He is finished with us. We buck, kick, scream, and run away from what God wants us to be. In the end we will get there, because we are mandated by God. Now, how we get there is left up to us.

Defected Before Birth

In my reading and studying, I've discovered that normally 97 out of 100 babies are born healthy; however, an expected mother has a 3 to 4 percent chance of giving birth to a child with defects. However, if defects run in the family then the chances are alarmingly higher. If your father dealt with the spirit of substance abuse, there's a high chance you will also deal with it. If your father was an abused person, there's a high chance you will deal with it too.

A birth defect is said to be a problem that a child is born with. I would like to say that a birth defect is a challenge that is present at the time of birth that the child being born has no control of or has anything to do with it. It came with the child's birth.

Now here's the thing about a birth defect. A birth defect can be so mild that on the outside the baby looks normal. It is not until testing has taken place that it can be discovered that something has gone off-center. It is the test that identifies or discovers that there's a defect.

In our lives we don't know what we are made of until we are tested. The test will identify or it will cause you to discover your weakness and your strength. Testing will let you know if there's a defect.

In the medical field there's a term called inborn defects, which is an abnormality or out of the norm birth. In other words, something happened while the child was still in the womb that was not detected. Defected in the womb, in the making process.

The same is true in our spiritual birth. Many of us are born with spiritual defects. These defects came from church teaching that were passed to us from our parents' faith or from the church environment that we were raised in. For this reason when we are born again we are born with lots of stuff, filled with error in our belief, believing that what we were taught or what our parents passed to us was correct. Now as born again believers we find ourselves having to unlearn many doctrines of error in order to relearn true doctrines.

R Born 2 X

The Bible states in I Cor 15:45-47 (KJV), "So it is written: "The first man Adam became a living being"; the last Adam, a life-giving spirit. Howbeit that was not first which is spiritual, but that which is natural; and afterward that which is spiritual. The first man was of the dust of the earth; the second man is of heaven.

In layman terms, Paul is establishing a principle, "First natural then spiritual". The natural is a blueprint for the spiritual. I first wanted to establish that what happens in the natural is a layout, a pattern or blueprint of what's happen in the spiritual. In saying that, what I'm saying is, any person who is born again, there is a high chance that while you were being born again, you were born again with some imperfection.

Because you are born again does not mean that you are perfect or correct in your faith or doctrines. Born again doesn't mean that you are absent of issues. In the natural 40% of defects comes from your parents or environment. Based on that principle, 40 % of my issues and yours come from the stuff that we had to deal with in our families or in our church environment, and truth be told, the church doesn't have an answer for all of my issues. Now the question is, "How do I deal with my issues when the church doesn't even have an answer for the issues and the areas of my brokenness?"

What happens if my brokenness is so mild that by looking at me I seem normal?

It is not until you have spent some time with me that you find out that there are some deep seeded wounds that I don't know where they came from. The Apostle has problems and he doesn't know how to get rid of them.

There are things that Paul asked God to remove from him, issues, problems, problems that needed to be solved. There are things I've asked God to remove from me. Problems that I was born again with. I can say like Paul, "That which I know to do I don't do and that I don't do, I do. I have a defect!" In other word, Lord I am a mess. But God said, "I know"! Not only does God know, He also said, "I have enough grace for that." You are broken but you are useable.

I don't know where you are in your spiritual walk. If you look close enough at yourself and become the man in the mirror, looking at the vessel that God created, you will discover that you were born with some imperfections.

We all were born in sin! We were shaped in iniquity! My sin may not be your sin but if you stick with any person long enough you will see some traces and some highlights of a person who is wounded with an issue or two. Broken but usable! I like to call it, "living with a challenge".

Living with a challenge

Challenge is to invite someone to do something that will be difficult to do within his own abilities and strength. Because we are living in a politically correct time, we no longer use the term handicapped, we now uses, "challenged or impaired".

Impaired is different from challenged. Impaired means being in a less than perfect or whole condition. So my hearing is impaired, my sight may be impaired. I think we are all less than perfect. However, challenging is living in this world with those imperfections and making the best out of it.

"And lest I should be exalted above measure through the abundance of the revelations, there was given to me a thorn in the flesh, the messenger of Satan to buffet me, lest I should be exalted above measure. For this thing I besought the Lord thrice, that it might depart from me. And he said unto me, My grace is sufficient for thee: for my strength is made perfect in weakness. Most gladly therefore will I rather glory in my infirmities, that the power of Christ may rest upon me. 2 Cor. 12:7-9(KJV)

Look at it from this point of view. I've lost my arms. Now I am challenged to do something that will be difficult to do, testing my abilities and strength to perform with people who have two arms. In other word, they have it all together. But isn't it strange that when you try to live for God, what you face are challenges. God never design things in your life to handicap you. God designs things in your life to see if you would be able to walk through life knowing something is wrong, yet making the best out of what you have.

God will use you with your challenge as in the case with Jonathan's son. "And Jonathan, Saul's son, had a son that was lame of his feet. He was five years old when the tidings came of Saul and Jonathan out of Jezreel, and his nurse took him up, and fled: and it came to pass, as she made haste to flee, that he fell, and became lame. And his name was Mephibosheth" (2 Samuel 4:4 KJV).

In a time of war, the enemy attacked the house of Jonathan and crushed his family. The mid-wife snatched up the boy and ran. In her haste to escape the killing, she dropped him. Quickly she picked him up again and ran to hide in terror. The child lived. But both his legs were broken and twisted. The bones never set right. All his life he was lame. All his life he was made to live with a challenge; not because of what he did or at any doing of his own. He was dropped!

There are many challenges in life that we lives with. Someone dropped you. It's not your fault that you live with this challenge. But remember, God will use things in your life to see if you will be able to walk through life knowing something is wrong.

God will use you with your challenge.

You can't live your entire life blaming others for your mishap. Maybe you were dropped. Maybe your parents weren't able to give you all the necessities of life. Maybe your dad was a drunk and your mother was a street girl. Maybe you were shaped by your environment. You will never move forward in life always looking back and blaming others. You have to take the bull by the horn and move on. Life isn't always fair, but God hasn't forgotten you. David restored his friend, Jonathan's son Mephibosheth, to his rightful place; at the King's table. There's a seat for you at the Master's table.

One day King David asked his servants if anyone from Jonathan's family survived, "That I may show the kindness of God unto him". The king drew Mephibosheth to him, restored his family's property and declared, "As for Mephibosheth, he shall eat at my table as one of my own sons for all his life". And that's what happened. The broken, twisted, lame man always ate at the king's own table as part of the family.

The broken man had done nothing to deserve this honor; he was included because of what someone else had done. He sat at the table, not because he was perfect, but because the King claimed him as family. We sat at the Master's table because of what Jesus has done. From the waist up, while setting at the Master's table, no one could seek his challenge. They all looked the same!

If you really look at it, the way life works out, it seems that every single one of us was dropped on our heads at birth! We live twisted, broken, lame lives and the bones never seem to set just right. Broken at birth, broken at life, and unfortunately all too often broken by choice.

How long can a person blame the childhood nurse for everything? We move and function, but with a limp. Some hurts visible, some invisible. But nevertheless, we live sin-broken, twisted, lamed lives. Yet, the Eternal King offers to show us the kindness of God. Not because of what we have accomplished but because of what Christ did.

Jesus invites us to His table. He said, "Behold I stand at the door and knock. If any man hear My voice and open the door, I will sup with him and him with Me". (Rev 3:20 KJV)

*The day you stop blaming others is the day
you will find out who you truly are.*

Used With Your Flaws

Tonex, the great gospel singer wrote a song that says: You know my other side. I can no longer hide. Let you down so many times. Sin freshly crucifies. Thought that I had a plan. I had it all figured out. But the more that you tried, to be by my side' the more I push you out. Lord make me over, Lord make me over.

As beautiful as the song is and the heart of this great singer cry's out to God to make him over again, God doesn't make us all "over again", as in the case with the potter and the vessel with the defect. There are some of us that God hand-picked to use with our defects, with our problem.

Some of us will always walk with a limp. Some of us will always be working to overcome a habit or a problem. There will always be something. The only way to move forward with a challenge is to never pretend that you don't have it. Red is red and you have to call it for what it is. Now here's the kicker. Confess it to God. God can handle what people can't. As far as I'm concern, the issue is not Tonex problem. The problem is people who knows about Tonex's problem and will not accept him because now they know the problem.

Here's the challenge. When you know you have a challenge you have to rearrange your life. When you know you have a substance abuse challenge, there are things you can't do and places you can't go. You have to rearrange by changing your environment or situation in your life because if you don't rearrange your life you'll keep bumping into the same stuff. You will keep falling over things and missing it again and again.

Allow me to say this. God spoke to me and said, "Son, I don't have a problem with your problems or your challenges, it's people who have a problem with Me using you with your problems.

*When you know you have a challenge
you have to rearrange your life.*

God doesn't look at our problems as we do or as others do. Where people see stress God sees opportunities. Where people see crisis, God sees growth and improvement. God's purpose in times of crisis and problems is to teach His children precious lessons. They are designed to educate, and build us up. And when we learn from them and ride out these storms of life, people will see the great hands of God at work.

We need to see the joy and opportunities through times of problems. We can learn to make our life joyful by grabbing the crisis and growing from it. To become the person that we are capable of being for our benefit and His glory. God wants to use our problems for good, to make us better and stronger for our personal development and in turn for us to be able to help others in their lives.

Not Good Enough

Do you ever feel that you are not good enough to be used by God? Well, I'm the first to say, "You are not good enough". "All of us have become like one who is unclean, and all our righteous acts are like filthy rags; we all shrivel up like a leaf, and like the wind our sins sweep us away" (Isaiah 64:6 KJV).

In my research, with much surprise, I discovered that the term "filthy rags" is quite strong in Hebrew. The word filthy literally means the bodily fluids from a woman's menstrual cycle. The word rags is a translation of begged, meaning a rag or garment. Therefore, our righteous acts are considered by God as offensive as a soiled feminine hygiene product. With all our righteousness, we are still not good enough.

My son made a statement about one of the members of the church. He stated, "Now this sister here, she's 'real saved'. Real saved? What was he saying? Was she one of those saints that get up early in the morning before dawn and pray an hour each morning? One who always have the right Bible verse on hand for a conversation? Never fight with her spouse? Fast twice a week? Pay tithes and offering? Don't smoke or drink alcohol? Well I'm definitely not that person. While I know that my heart is on a path of sanctification, I still never feel "good enough" to be used by God. God dorsn't use us because we are good enough. God uses us because of our availability.

Stop telling me I'm not good enough. I know that, but right now I'm doing the best I can.

Often I become overbearing with this mental picture of the kind of person that God uses and I don't see me. The Lord spoke to my spirit saying, "You don't have to be perfect for Me to use you, be usable. If I used your abilities, people would say it's you. If I use you because you are usable, people would know it's Me. Here's what I love about God. God knows that I am inadequate. He knows all about me, after all He created me. When God use people like you and me, God is showing us and others, how great He is. God is saying, "You may be inadequate but I Am not.""

Who God Can't Use

There are some people who God will not use. In reading the 21st chapter of Leviticus God is giving instruction as to who is qualified to serve Him in the Tabernacle. With all of the thoughtfulness training that is given by God in this structure as to how to use proper material and what needs to be in the holy place and in the holy of holy and how there needs to be an adequate entrance way, here of all places in the Word, God seem to discriminate against people who have issues. People who He will not use.

In this chapter God uses an unlikely source. God tells Moses that these are the people who cannot work for me in the church. These are the people who can't bring the offering, who can't stand on my behalf. These are the people who do not meet the standard. These are people that are messed up. When I read this, these are the people that sounds like me.

Leviticus 21:16-23 (KJV) "16. The LORD said to Moses, 17. "Say to Aaron: (Aaron is Moses blood brother, both from the Levi tribe)"For the generations to come none of your descendants who has a defect may come near to offer the food of his God. 18. No man who has any defect may come near: no man who is blind or lame, disfigured or deformed; 19. No man with a crippled foot or hand, 20. Or who is hunchbacked or dwarfed, or who has any eye defect, or who has festering or running sores or damaged testicles. 21. No descendant of Aaron the priest who has any defect is to come near to present the offerings made to the LORD by fire. He has a defect; he must not come near to offer the food of his God. 22. He may eat the most holy food of his God, as well as the holy food; 23. Yet because of his defect, (Because he's not perfect) he must not go near the curtain or approach the altar, and so desecrate my sanctuary. I am the LORD, who makes them holy.

In an earlier chapter we established the fact that it's first natural than spiritual. God is establishing a spiritual principle as to those who He will use. Now here's the kicker, the person God told to tell other folks that they were messed up, was messed up himself. He told Moses, who had a stammering tongue.

Moses was raised in a house he knew he didn't belong in. He was in foster care after his own mother gave him up and his father was nowhere to be found. He was a murder. Yet God used an imperfect man to tell others that because of their imperfection He couldn't use them.

God is God! He will use somebody that's messed up to tell me what's wrong with you. God uses broken vessels to tell us about our brokenness. But we have the nerve to complain about the broken vessel that deliver the message to us, but can't even identify the brokenness that's inside of us.

God is amazing in His selection of messengers; he understands that it takes one to know one. He understands that sometimes the only person that can get to the drug addict is someone who used to be addicted or is still battling with addiction. I believe that God will put somebody in front of us with all of their issues just so you can see what yours are.

Blind: To have no sight. So God says to Moses, these are the people that you can't use for my kingdom, these are the people who are messed up, and these are the people who have missed the mark. The people who are blind I don't want them representing me. Please don't limit that to the physical. Blind mean without vision.

There is something to be said about people who claim to love God but have no vision for their lives. Too many of us are satisfied with the right now, while God is pointing to a greater way and a greater possibility. So many of us have shared the vision that God has given us to folks who try to talk us out of it because they can't see what God is showing us. You have to get away from people who are blind, because all they're looking at is now. When you've been anointed by God, you can't be stuck in what you see now. Now is not your future. We walk by faith and not by sight.

Lame: To walk unevenly. God can't use people who just sit by the pool. In John Chapter five there's a pool called Bethesda and right by the pool there were lame folk and Jesus came out of nowhere and said "how come you're not walking and a lame man complained and said, "I had nobody to push me in the pool" God says, "That's the kind of folk I'm talking about. People who always blame others for their uneven life.

The only thing worse than being blind is having eyes but having no vision.

I'm sick of being around people who keep blaming other people for why they're not further along in life. If it wasn't for my parents. If it wasn't for my wife or husband. If it wasn't, if it wasn't. You've got to learn to stop depending on other people and learn to depend on God and what God has placed inside of you. People will let you down but never God. People will make promises and say that they're going to be there, but when times get tough you'll find out that you're in it all by yourself. No more excuse making!

If you live long enough you will find out that people will walk away from you in your most vulnerable moment. You need to learn to encourage yourself. There comes a time when you have to say to God, "Lord, it's just me, myself, I and You."

I am not depending on anyone to do anything for me. If I can't get it I'm going to trust God to give me the resources and help I need. Stop blaming other people! Stop acting like a victim and start acting like a victor! Stop playing the blame game and say "I can do all things through Christ that strengthens me!"

Broken Feet: Psalms declares, "Blessed is the man who walketh not in the council of the ungodly nor standeth in the way of sinners." God is saying, "I don't want people who keep going back to what I delivered them from". You cried when you were in the middle of it and God delivered you from it and every time we turn around you're back in it.

When God shuts the door you better change your address. Get your number changed. Move in another direction. Move out of town. There is a time when you have to walk away from some stuff, away from some folk. It is not personal, it's business. You've got to get what God has for you and if someone is draining you and stressing you out and worrying and fighting you, blocking you from your goal, you better tell them to get stepping before they get walked over. God can't use people with broken feet, who keep going back to what they've been delivered from.

Broken Hands. Anyone with a broken hand doesn't have the capacity to hold on. I don't know where you are in this stage of your life, but this is the season where God wants you to hold on. I know you've thought about quitting. I know that there have been times where you've said it just ain't worth it. I know there were moments when you almost gave up on God and almost gave up on the church but God says when you get to the end of your rope, tie a knot and hold on. And if you can't hold on, let go and fall in God's arms. He's able to catch you.

Hunchback: someone who has a large round part on their back that is caused by an unusual curve in their spine. God said, "I also don't want anybody working for me with a Hunchback". Being a spiritual hunchback is a sign that they can't handle the weight. They're bent over from their circumstances. God needs people that while they have the weight of the world on their shoulders, you can't tell by looking at them. There is someone today who is carrying pounds of stress but you don't wear it on your face and in your performance. As a matter of fact you look better than what you're going through. You're not trying to be a part of a fashion show, you just had to let the enemy know that you didn't break me. He didn't take your joy. He didn't take your pride. You're still standing even when you felt broken on the inside.

Sometimes God will allow the enemy to put a weight on your back, as with Job, to show the devil that you can stand under the pressure. So many people in your family, people that you grew up with, people you used to run with have fallen by the wayside because they couldn't handle the pressure. When life got hard they got swallowed up in drugs and swallowed up on the streets and swallowed up by alcoholism and depression. But when the pressure started mounting, you refused to lay down and play dead.

"No temptation has overtaken you but such as is common to man; and God is faithful, who will not allow you to be tempted beyond what you are able, but with the temptation will provide the way of escape also, that you may be able to endure it" (1 Cor. 10:13 KJV).

Dwarfs: small; to make somebody or something else seem very small or very unimportant by comparison. Let's not look at this in the physical, let's look at it in the Spiritual. I don't want anybody who refuses to grow into their full potential. Anyone who cuts off where they're supposed to be by small thinking and a small perspective and a small mindset. You were created to be a giant!

The place that you're operating in is too small for you. The doors are too small for your blessings. That check that they're paying you don't match your anointing. The people that's surrounding you, you've outgrown them and they can't catch up to where you're going. Stop hanging out with people of small mind setting. You were created to hand with giants but you keep limiting yourself with dwarf thinking.

Are you tired of low living, small planning and the ordinary? Are you tired of a smaller than normal management? Do you want to grow past where you are? I don't have time to spend with folk who want to stay at the same level. If you don't want more for your life you will never be an asset to the kingdom. If you don't think you can get better than life is right now you will never see the fullness of God's glory. People who have dwarf thinking don't understand people who think outside of the box.

As a man thinketh so is he. I don't have ten dollar thoughts, hundred dollar thoughts. I have million dollar thoughts because I serve a great big God. I know folks keep telling you, "Slow down, you're doing too much. Why you going after all of that? If I was you I would be satisfied". Well, you ain't me! And because you ain't me you don't understand me. I want more! And on top of that, I can't have a wife who act like Snow White, hanging out with the seven dwarfs. I am a giant so Dr Sarah have to be a giant keeper!

Running Sores: sores that will not heal. God told Moses that He didn't want anyone who has Running Sores. Wounds and scabs that won't heal from something in the past. They keep dragging on for years with things that God has already delivered them from. Every time you talk to them they keep talking about the pain of the past, because they won't allow God to heal them from it. You can't move forward always looking back. So they didn't say they were sorry. Get over it, let go, and move on.

God is looking for someone who can say, "Yes, I've been hurt, I've been wounded, I went through some painful experiences, I was in some stuff that almost killed me, but that was then, and this is now. I'm not telling you to pretend like you've never been hurt before, but you've got to make up in your mind that if it didn't kill you, it made you stronger. If it didn't wipe you out, God wanted you to get a lesson out of it.

Crushed Testicles: seeds that will not produce. God is looking for you to reproduce. God can't use anyone who won't be productive, who doesn't have the ability to reproduce, and who only wants self-fulfillment. People who's not looking to see how they can be a blessing to others but everything is about what's in it for them. We shouldn't be the only ones in our family with faith. Our faith should be catching so that people in our circle will catch on. The enemy wants to crush your spirit so that you'll never produce.

So the Scriptures say that if you're messed up like these folk, you can't be used by God, you're not fit for the Kingdom, you're not suited to take over. But then He leaves a "Legal Loophole". God says, "Unless your Father is Aaron than you can obtain the blessings". 22. "He may eat the most holy food of his God, as well as the holy food". I might not can do what you can do because of my challenge, but I can still get the same blessing from God. We both eat from the Master's Table! We eat the same bread.

If this being the case, learn from the fact that you're messed up, but because of who "Your Father is", you can still receive the blessing, become clean and you can serve. Because your father is God, you can become clean and God can use you. I'm so thankful that as messed up as I am, I know who my Father is.

I often remind myself that I am where I am, not because I'm so good but because of God's grace. I can write a whole book on that. As a matter of fact when I want to talk about his grace there's only one thing I can say about it, it's miraculous!

With all of my brokenness God still use me. In spite of all of the things that was and is still wrong with me, God has a purpose for my life. The enemy is a dirty fighter, he tried to do everything to mess me up. He wanted to make sure that I didn't meet the mandate of God. I may be broken but I am still usable.

That's why I praise Him. If you knew all my issues, all my mess, everything that's wrong with me and how God loved me anyway, you would give Him the glory too because of the grace of God.

God doesn't just want perfect people. He wants usable people. Perfect people don't know how to bring a sacrifice. Now God want people who are wounded and broken and are hurt but understand that God can redeem them and yes God can use them. If You can use "ANYTHING" Lord, You can use me.

I may not be good enough for people, but
I'm good enough to be used by God.

†

THE BOOK OF ADAMS

CHAPTER XVII

That's Behind Me Now

Joshua 8: 1-2 KJV "Then the Lord said to Joshua, "Do not be afraid; do not be discouraged. Take the whole army with you, and go up and attack Ai. For I have delivered into your hands the king of Ai, his people, his city and his land. You shall do to Ai and its king as you did to Jericho and its king, except that you may carry off their plunder and livestock for yourselves.""

The Adams' family have fought many battles and won each and every one of them. All we had ever experienced was victory. V.I.C.T.O.R.Y! We lived and walked in it. We fought the spirit of death over our mother with an issue of blood, and won. We fought the spirit of death over our youngest sister, and won. We fought the spirit of death over our dad, and won. As a thirteen year old boy, I fought the spirit of death over myself, used the name of Jesus, and won. We have survived many years of hardship and trouble. Miracles lived in our life!

My father followed and taught us to practice and follow the miracle ministry of A. A. Allen. We believed in signs, wonders and miracles. We experienced the miracles of Elijah. When doctors said they would have to operate, we prayed and God always delivered. We had the miracle of Peter and Jesus; when they need money and there was none. God blew money down the street once and we survived. We had faced the walls of Jericho in our lives, gave God praise and the walls fell down. Just to name a few. We were known as the faith and miracle family.

To be truthful about it, I took much pride in having the hands of God upon my family. My first defeat, that I can recall, came at the death of my twin brother. Blew me away. Prayed and he still died; never had we been here before. We always won! At the age of fifty he died from heart failure.

Divorced my wife after thirty-three years of marriage; never been here before. Always knew how to work through bad situations and win. Divorce won. Sister died at the age of forty–seven; never been here before. Oldest brother died at the age of fifty-nine from heart failure; never been here before. Dad and mom went home to be with the Lord. Mom died in a nursing home alone in the wee hours of the night. Only Jesus to comfort her. Dad died at home alone in his home with only Jesus by his side; never been here before. I've made lots of bad decisions and tons of mistakes. Lost battles! How do you bounce back? How do I let go of what's behind me?

I truly understand Joshua. He had survived many years as a slave in Egypt. He lived through and experienced the ten plauges that God brought upon Egypt. He had crossed the Red Sea and survived 40 years in the wilderness. He had crossed the Jordon River and had defeated the city of Jericho. Victory was his first name. After a great victory at Jericho comes Joshua's first defeat. He faced Ai and failed. He lost the battle! Joshua went from victory to defeat.

In life, everything will not go your way

The Bible said that Joshua was afraid. Not only was he afraid for being in no-man-land, he was also discouraged, having a lack of courage to fight again because of the fear of failure. What do you do when you fall from victory to defeat, from winning to losing, from success to setback? Do you stop? Do you go back? Do you retreat back to where you came? Do you go back to doing what you use to do?

When my twin died I stopped praying for people. I went into a shutdown mode. I stopped fasting. I was afraid to pray for people because of my defeat; I prayed, he died. Now I was afraid that others would die. What was I to do? Do I live in my sorrow or do I attack again. Do I pray again? Do I trust God again? Do I begin again and let the past be the past?

I've discovered in life that everything is not going to go your way. You will not get everything you want. Everyone you pray for will not receive healing. You will not win every battle you fight. You will fail sometimes; however, failure is not final. You can begin again. God is a second chance God.

God gave Joshua a second chance to attack Ai, after his failure. God told Joshua, "Do not be afraid; do not be discouraged. Take the whole army with you, and go up and attack Ai again". Your failures are behind you. The past doesn't exist. Attack again!

"Do not be afraid: do not be discouraged." Fear is the greatest enemy to your faith. Fear is to be frightened of somebody or something or about taking action. My fear came about because I thought that miracles, signs and wonders was based upon me and my righteousness. After the death of my twin, I thought I wasn't good enough. Maybe it's because of me and something I've done wrong that this happened.

We often put too much on us that God never required. We are not the miracle worker. It is God who heals the sick not you and me. Our righteousness is never good enough to be use by God. As a matter of fact, we have no righteousness. The righteousness that we operate in is not ours, it belongs to God.

You will make bad decisions and you will make many mistakes. I had to learn that mistakes are not all bad. Mistakes are lessons learned. There's good in your mistakes. Mistakes are good for you. Mistakes let you know that you are human and are subject to failures. There's only one that was and is perfect. His name is Jesus

If one is to move forward after a mistake, one need to first take the courage to look at a mistake for what it is. A mistake is a mishap, something that didn't go the way you wanted, tired, or planned for it to go. It just happened while you were trying to do something else. It's an accident. You weren't trying to do wrong, but you did wrong. You weren't trying to miss the ball, but you did. When you got up to bat it was your intention, and you tried to hit, but you struck out. You did wrong while trying to do good.

> *Mistakes let you know that you are*
> *human and are subject to failures.*

To admit to your wrong, willfully doing it or through a mistake, is the first step to victory from your past. Why is this so important you asked? Well, if you don't know what you did was wrong you could do it again. Discover what happened. What did I do to make the mistake? Joshua discovered what was wrong. Sin was in the camp. Once the sin was dealt with and removed, God gave them victory. God didn't give up on him and God has not given up on you because of your past failures and mistakes.

God didn't give up on people and God won't give up on you. You will have to rebel and quit! If you rebel and quit, it's not God who gave up, it you. It's still there where you quit at. We all have made foolish mistakes. When the word of the Lord came to Joshua "the second time" it came with the same assignment he had received the first time, take Ai! It was God's first plan for Joshua to go and take Ai; it was still God's plan for Joshua to take Ai. God's plan for Joshua did not change and God plan for you has not changed. God said, "I have not changed My mind about you; attack Ai."

Same Assignment

In the book of Jonah, chapter 1, God said to Jonah, "Arise, go to Nineveh, that great city, and cry out against it; for their wickedness has come up before Me." God gave Jonah an assignment, a particular task, a particular job. Go to Nineveh and cry out against that city because of their sins. Jonah didn't do what God had commanded. "But Jonah arose to flee to Tarshish from the presence of the Lord. He went down to Joppa, and found a ship going to Tarshish; so he paid the fare, and went down into it, to go with them to Tarshish from the presence of the Lord (Jonah 1:2 KJV).

Jonah ran from the presence of God because he didn't want to do this assignment. How many times have we ran from God's presence because we didn't want to do what He asked of us? Every assignment is not easy; however, when God gives you an assignment, it's yours! Did God give up on Jonah because he ran away from Him instead of running toward Him? No! God has not giving up on you. You still have an assignment do.

God will chase you down. Jonah found out that his legs were too short to out run God. God will do and use whatever He has to in order to get you to your expected end. God brought trouble into the life of Jonah. "But the Lord sent out a great wind on the sea, and there was a mighty tempest on the sea, so that the ship was about to be broken up (Jonah 1:4 KJV)".

Jonah thought he had gotten away from his "God sent assignment". You may run but you can't hide. Your assignment is still awaiting you. What you have found comfort in, thinking it has you covered, God will break it down! In the bottom of the ship Jonah found comfort. While sleeping in the midst of his comfort, God sent a storm and broke up his comfort zone.

Your legs are too short to out run God

As a preacher's kid, I am mandated by God to preach His Word. From the womb of my mother and loin of my father it came. God "called" my parents from a lifestyle of sin. My mother was a dancer on the ballroom floor. My father was a bootlegger. God called him into the ministry. Through their calling I was born into this ministry, mandated and authorized by God to live a godly lifestyle, and preach the Word on a public platform, because of the calling He placed on my parents.

As a young and foolish boy, I tried my best to run from this platform of ministry. There were other things I wanted to do and preaching wasn't on my list. At the age of sixteen I left home trying to run from God's assignment on my life. There among my peers, hiding in the comfort of a crowd, I was called out by another young man to lead prayer and join the Bible class. Of all the people there, why did they ask me? What did they see on me that others didn't see?

I ran from there into another state, hundreds of miles away. There in the comfort of my home, away from everyone I knew, I thought I had out run my assignment. Lying in my bed one day, I could hear singing coming from the outside. I knew that sound, it was the sound of praise and worship, the same sound I was running from.

Afraid to open the front door, I went, through the back door, around the house, to see what was going on. There outside my apartment a small group was having street meeting, singing and preaching, in my front yard. I stood in the back of the crowd wondering, "Why did they have to mess up my day, of all the places why my front yard?"

All of a sudden, unexpected for it to come, the preacher pointed directly to me, behind everyone there and said, "Son, you are a backslider, God has an assignment for you!" Oh no, not here! Where can I go? Where can I hide? King David said, "If I make my bed in hell, He's there." No place to hide.

You may run but you can't hid.

I ran for years, joined the navy, and got involved in drugs, trying to run from God's presence. I can recall once, while doing LSD, looking in a glass of wine tripping, God knocked me off of my high. There in that glass of wine my father appeared to me preaching saying, "Son, God's calling you!"

For five years I ran from God's presence and His mandate on my life. With drugs filling my veins, longing for a fix, I rededicated my life to God one night in the city of Chicago. God hadn't changed His mind about me. My assignment was the same. Preach the Gospel of Jesus Christ. I discovered that when there's a calling or a mandate on your life, your legs are too short to out run it. Surrender!

Jonah discovered this in the bottom of the ship. God caused trouble to come upon Jonah and those aboard the ship. For the saving of the ship Jonah was casted off in the midst of the sea. There God had prepared a huge fish to swallow him up; after three days in the belly of the fish Jonah surrendered to his calling. God didn't change His mind about Jonah. His assignment was the same. "Arise, go to Nineveh, that great city, and cry out against it; for their wickedness has come up before Me."

Jonah made a mistake. He messed up. He ran from the presence of God. He ran from his calling. But God, restored him to his proper place and gave Jonah a second chance. The past was over and now it was time to move forward. Leave your past in the past!

Mistakes are lessons learned.

You may ask, "Why do we need to leave the past in the past?" Well, first and for most, it is because it doesn't exist. It's gone forever. We blew the first one but God gave us another chance. We made a mistake. We made bad choices, and yes, we have to live with that. We all have past regrets, and many are saying, "If I could only go back in time, if I could do it again, and differently, I'll be a different person. You can't unscramble eggs! You can't go back! That's why you have to leave the past in the past. It's behind you now and for those who always want to remind you of you past, leave them where you found them. In your past!

I had to learn that in this life mistakes are part of the process of my growth and development. It comes with life. They are part of trials and errors. When we as "believers" recognize the certainty of mistakes, and that they are part of the ongoing experiment which life is, then we can relax more. We don't set out to make them but they are sure to happen.

Forgive Yourself

In our prayers we pray, "Lord forgive me as I forgive others". How about, "Lord forgive me as I forgive myself"? Forgiving yourself is just as important as you forgiving others. There is a part of us that have a tendency to hold ourselves more accountable than we do others. We can justify forgiving others, even for a terrible offense, yet we seem to find no justification for forgiving ourselves for an equal or lesser offense. God forgives us so why is it hard for us to forgive ourselves?

I truly believe that we as believers believe that there's a price, some form of life-long self-punishment that we have to pay for our mistakes.

We believe that forgiving ourselves is not even a consideration because most of us think that we must hold ourselves in a state of constant remembrance, lest we forget.

We are to practice following God's ways. He is our example. On that note we must remember that when God forgives us, it is stated in Jeremiah 31:34 that He remembers our sins no more. This does not mean that our all-knowing God forgets, but rather, because He forgives us, He chooses not to bring up our sin in a negative way. If God forgives us, truly we are to forgive ourselves. It is just as important to forgive ourselves as it is to forgive others.

Letting Go Of Negative People

There are many things in life I had to unlearn in order to relearn. I learned that I had to let go of people who wanted to hold things over my head, for a life time, because of my mistakes. I've learned that you don't have to pay and repay, over and over again for your past. When a person truly forgives you, they may not ever forget the offence; however, they will not use it in a negative way against you.

I also had to learn that forgiving doesn't mean forgetting. I thought that by some miracle that after I forgave others, or forgave myself, that I had to or would "forget" what happened. Forgiving yourself is not about forgetting. We need to remember so that we don't repeat the same thing again. Forgiving yourself is simply about letting go of what you are holding against yourself so that you can move on with God. If God has moved on, we should do the same. It's behind you now! Go and attack again!

Life is full of choices. I chose to live, let the past be the past, forgive myself and attack again. I have decided that every choice that I have made in life will take me to my expected end, be it good or bad. We cannot afford to allow our mistakes to rob us of the opportunity to be a life-giving individual.

By no means misunderstand what I am saying. Forgiving ourselves does not let us off the hook, it does not justify what we have done, wrong is wrong; however, it is not final and you are not finish because of it. Forgiving my self was a choice for me. It took much courage and strength.

Forgiving myself gave me the opportunity to become an overcomer rather than live in a state of guilt, where church people wanted me to live, being a victim of my own scorn by disliking and disrespecting what God had forgiven.

How can you forgive others when you can't forgive yourself? You can only give what you have. Hurting people hurt others. Truth be told, I nor you can change what has happened. You cannot restore lives to where they were before the event. However, you can make a difference in you now. I had to forgive myself so healing could begin in my life. Forgiving me has changed my complete direction in life and it will change yours too.

Man in the Mirror

Look at the man in the mirror. Do you look in the mirror at yourself, but don't like the person you see? If that be the case, then you need to forgive yourself. Learn how to love the person that God has made! Because of what happened to me as a child, being molested and used by others, I hated myself. This is what is called a stronghold, or an incorrect thinking pattern that needed to be torn down in my mind. I had to learn to love me; the creation that God had made.

There's a new you coming forth! If you have repented of your sins, and taken them before the Lord, then you are forgiven. Now, right now, you are new. The past is gone! The devil doesn't want you to come to realize the power of that. Stop associating your failures with your "new creation" made in the image of God. God's Word says, "2 Corinthians 5:17 KJV, "Therefore if any man be in Christ, he is a new creature: old things are passed away; behold all things are become new."

Look at the person in the mirror and tell yourself, "I love you" and mean it with your heart. I'm not talking about a prideful way, but a humble means of accepting who God has formed in you. Love and accept the person that Christ has made in you, and forgive yourself as Christ has forgiven you. Remember, you may be broken but you are usable!